Glaube Spiele Hoffnung

Hope and Play

Die wundersame Entstehung der Oberammergauer Passion 2022

The magical making of the Oberammergau Passion Play 2022

Sebastian Beck
Christiane Lutz

Hope and Play

The magical making of the Oberammergau Passion Play 2022

Glaube Spiele Hoffnung

Die wundersame Entstehung der Oberammergauer Passion 2022

Süddeutsche Zeitung Edition

Inhalt
Content

7	Wie alles begann / *How it all started*
8	Fotostrecke: Die Vorbereitungen / *Photo series: The Preparations*
26	Der Mann am Kreuz / *The Man on the Cross*
38	Porträt Eva-Maria Reiser / *Portrait Eva-Maria Reiser*
40	Die Reise der 37 Apostel / *The Journey of the 37 Apostles*
54	Porträt Cengiz Görür / *Portrait Cengiz Görür*
56	Porträt Barbara Schuster / *Portrait Barbara Schuster*

58	Stückls Plan und Gottes Beitrag *Stückl's Plan and God's Contribution*	118	Interview mit Christian Stückl *Interview with Christian Stückl*
96	Porträt Abdullah Kenan Karaca *Portrait Abdullah Kenan Karaca*	128	Ein Dorf von Welt – Was Oberammergau so besonders macht *The Metropolitan Village – what makes Oberammergau so special*
98	Porträt Ursula Mayr *Portrait Ursula Mayr*		
100	Vom Gelübde zum Welttheater *From the Vow to World Theatre*	138	Porträt Christian Bierling *Portrait Christian Bierling*
112	Porträt Gabriele Weinfurter-Zwink *Portrait Gabriele Weinfurter-Zwink*	140	Fotostrecke: Endlich auf der Bühne *Photo series: Finally on Stage*
114	Porträt Peter Stückl *Portrait Peter Stückl*	159	Danksagung *Acknowledgements*
116	Haarige Angelegenheit *Hairy Affairs*	160	Impressum und Bildnachweis *Imprint and Credits*

Christiane Lutz

ist Redakteurin im Feuilleton der Süddeutschen Zeitung. Sie schreibt über Theater, Literatur und Glaubensthemen.

is an editor in the culture section of the Süddeutsche Zeitung. She writes about theatre, literature and subjects of faith.

Sebastian Beck

arbeitet seit 1987 für die Süddeutsche Zeitung und leitet den Bayernteil. Er fotografiert seit seiner Kindheit.

has worked for the Sueddeutsche Zeitung since 1987 and is head of the Bavaria section. Ever since his childhood, he has loved to take photos.

Wie alles begann

How it all started

The best thing about journalism is, that you can stick your nose into everything. So, why be content with just watching, when you can also be an active part of something really big happening? When Christiane Lutz asked Christian Stückl in spring 2017, when the preparations for the Passion Play 2020 would start, he grinned and said: "They have been going on for a while." Could we be part of it all? From the beginning? A photographer, a reporter? "Sure, why not?" So, there we were.

We were there, when the parts were announced, there for the beard decree even, hiked with the actors through desert valleys in Israel, were singing Hebrew songs on the bus, learned about Oberammergau's traditions as well as culinary insider tips, and met a bunch of great people, who tolerated us with stoic composure. We were there, too, when the play was canceled in 2020, and just as shocked as all the locals. Back then, it was far from clear, if this book could ever be finished. Taking the project back out of the drawer this fall, felt like going down into an untidy basement. Shall we finish it up?

And now, both things are ready – the book and the Passion Play. Salvation, in a way, mostly for the people of Oberammergau, but a little bit for us, too.

Das Schönste am Journalismus ist, dass man seine Nase überall reinstecken darf. Warum sich also mit dem Zuschauen begnügen, wenn man auch dabei sein kann, wie etwas ganz Großes entsteht? Als Christiane Lutz im Frühjahr 2017 Christian Stückl fragte, wann denn die Vorbereitungen zur Passion 2020 losgehen würden, grinste er und sagte: „Die laufen längst". Ob wir uns dranhängen dürften? Von Anfang an? Ein Fotograf, eine Reporterin? „Ja, warum nicht." Da hingen wir also.

Wir waren bei der Spielerverkündung dabei, bei sogar zwei Barterlässen, sind mit den Spielerinnen und Spielern durch israelische Wüstentäler gewandert, sangen hebräische Lieder im Bus, lernten Oberammergauer Bräuche, gastronomische Geheimtipps und eine Menge toller Menschen kennen, die uns mit stoischer Gelassenheit ertragen haben. Auch bei der Absage der Spiele 2020 waren wir dabei, genauso schockiert wie die Oberammergauer. Ob das Buch jemals vollendet werden würde, war damals alles andere als klar. Das Projekt im Herbst 2021 dann wieder hervorzuholen, fühlte sich an, wie in einen unaufgeräumten Keller hinabzusteigen. Wollen wir's zu Ende bringen?

Und jetzt ist beides da, das Buch und die Passion. Die Erlösung, gewissermaßen. Vor allem für die Oberammergauer. Ein bisschen aber auch für uns.

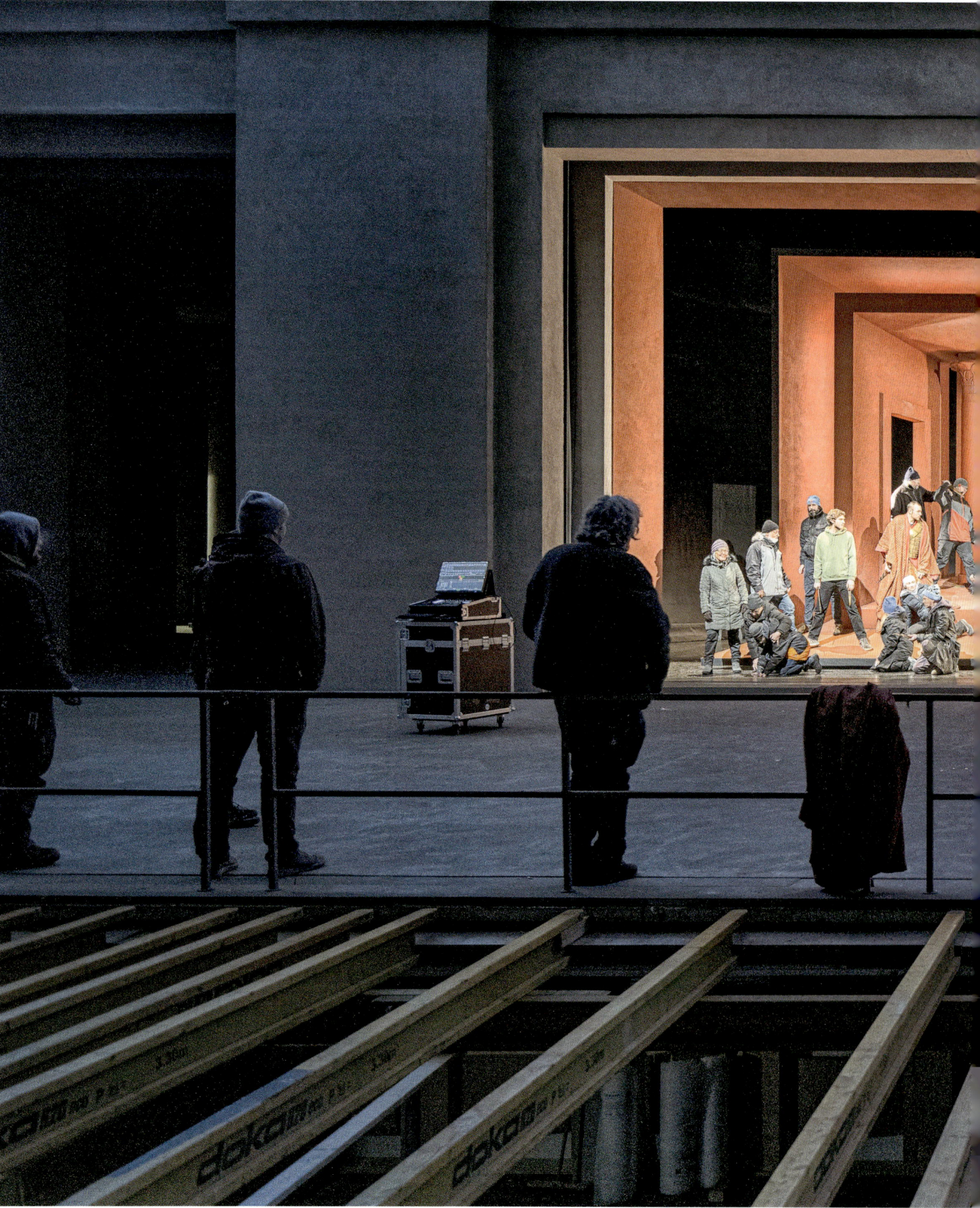

Der Mann am Kreuz

The Man on the Cross

»Die Rolle ist ein totales Geschenk.«

Jesus-Darsteller Frederik Mayet

»The role is a total gift.«

Jesus actor Frederik Mayet

Dreimal Jesus im Österreichischen Hospiz in Jerusalem (links). Rochus Rückel und Frederik Mayet beim zweiten Barterlass 2022 (oben).

Three times Jesus in the Austrian hospice in Jerusalem (left). Rochus Rückel and Frederik Mayet at the second beard decree 2022 (above).

Frederik Mayet on Jesus and what it's like to play him

Der Heiland und sein Vieh: Frederik Mayet lernt den Passions-Esel kennen.

The savior and his cattle: Frederik Mayet meets the Passion Play donkey.

I never wanted to be Jesus. I mean, that was never on my agenda as one of my aims in life. And now, I play him for the second time. After I got the part in 2010, the first thing I felt was pure euphoria, everybody came to me, patted my shoulder, congratulated me, and we laughed together. The next day, I woke up and was totally overwhelmed. For weeks, I was really insecure and felt low. From one day to the next, you are a person of public interest, everyone wants to know, who the new Jesus is. I felt this as a huge responsibility, a burden. It was too much.

At some point, one of my friends told me: "Fredi, you walk around town like a beaten dog. Why can't you be happy about it, enjoy it, you are going to be great." Then, I watched everything about Jesus, films about the passion of Christ, "Jesus Christ Superstar", I read books, the Bible, too. At some point, I understood, that it's always an interpretation. And we also show one.

Optically, Jesus was there very early in my life as a carved wooden figure. My history with the Passion Play began in 2000 when I was 20 and played the disciple John. Back then, I totally admired the actors who played Jesus, they were my role models. I loved being on stage with them. And now, all of a sudden, I am one of them.

Crazy things happen to you when you play Jesus. You travel a lot, you are on Australian TV-Shows, your picture is in the "Playboy", you meet politicians, VIPs, artists, and people from the economy. In 2010, Angela Merkel, then German Chancellor, came to my dressing room once to say hello and we took a picture. She left, I undressed, then suddenly she came back in, said she wanted to make a quick, undisturbed phone call. I was standing there in my underpants. And she said, very coolly: "Don't worry and keep changing your clothes. I won't look." I also had very strange encounters with evangelical US-Americans who couldn't really separate me, the actor, from my role. They wanted me to bless them. This form of religiousness is not really my thing just as any overidentification with my role. Still, all things considered, this role is a wonderful gift.

When the Passion Play was canceled in March 2020, I was in shock. Just like the rest of the world, I fell into a big hole of sadness and insecurity. The role of Jesus I had to put aside for a while, and at some point, I also wanted to cut my hair and shave my beard, but not right away. Today, I read the text differently, and ask more questions about health, death, and illness. I wonder why resources are so unfairly distributed in society, think about conflicts and wars. These themes are also present in the

Am Kreuz zu hängen ist ganz schön anstrengend.

Hanging on the cross is really strenuous.

Frederik Mayet über Jesus und wie es ist, ihn zu spielen

Ich wollte nie Jesus werden. Das heißt, ich hatte das nie auf meiner Liste als großes Lebensziel. Und jetzt spiele ich ihn zum zweiten Mal. Nach der Ernennung 2010 spürte ich erst totale Euphorie, alle kamen zu mir, klopften mir auf die Schulter, Glückwünsche, Gelächter. Am nächsten Tag bin ich aufgewacht und war völlig überfordert. Wochenlang schlich ich mit gebeugtem Kopf durchs Dorf. Von einem Tag auf den anderen bist du Person des öffentlichen Interesses, jeder will wissen, wer der neue Jesus ist. Ich habe eine große Verantwortung gespürt, eine Last. Es war zu viel.

Ein Freund sagte irgendwann: „Fredi, du gehst durchs Dorf wie ein geschlagener Hund, freu dich doch, genieß es, du kriegst es hin." Ich schaute dann alles über Jesus an, Passionsfilme, „Jesus Christ Superstar", las Bücher, die Bibel. Irgendwann habe ich verstanden, dass das alles immer Interpretation ist. Und wir zeigen auch eine.

Die optische Begegnung mit Jesus als geschnitztem Herrgott war in meinem Leben schon früh da. Meine Geschichte mit der Passion aber begann so richtig mit 20 Jahren, 2000 spielte ich den Jünger Johannes. Damals hatte ich eine totale Bewunderung für die Jesusdarsteller, das waren meine Vorbilder, ich habe es geliebt, mit ihnen auf der Bühne zu stehen. Und dann wurde ich plötzlich selbst einer.

Als Jesus erlebst du verrückte Sachen, verreist, trittst in australischen TV-Shows auf, stehst im „Playboy", triffst Politiker, Prominente, Künstler und Wirtschaftsleute. 2010 hat mich die damalige Bundeskanzlerin Angela Merkel mal in der Garderobe begrüßt vor der Vorstellung, wir haben ein Foto gemacht. Sie ging, ich zog mich aus, dann kam sie plötzlich wieder rein, sie wollte kurz ungestört telefonieren. Ich in der Unterhose. Sie, ganz cool: „Ziehen Sie sich ruhig weiter um, ich schau auch nicht hin." Skurril waren Begegnungen mit evangelikalen Amerikanern, die nicht recht zwischen Rolle und meiner Person trennen konnten. Die wollten, dass ich sie segne. Mit so einer Religiosität kann ich gar nichts anfangen und jede Überidentifikation mit der Rolle ist mir total fremd. Aber bei allen Entbehrungen: Die Rolle ist ein totales Geschenk.

Die Absage der Spiele im März 2020 war ein Schock. Sie hat mich in eine große Traurigkeit gestürzt und in eine Unsicherheit, wie die ganze Welt auch. Den Jesus musste ich dann erst mal beiseitelegen. Irgendwann, nicht gleich, wollte ich mir auch die Haare wieder abschneiden, den Bart rasieren. Ich lese den Text heute anders, stelle mir mehr Fragen über Gesundheit, Tod, Krankheit. Darüber, wie ungerecht die Mittel in der Gesellschaft verteilt sind. Konflikte, ja Kriege. Diese

Der Einzug nach Jerusalem, die erste große Szene der Passion.

The entry into Jerusalem, the first major scene of the Passion Play.

Passion Play, Jesus talks about these things. When you read the text, you can also hear harsh criticism of the pope and the church, which is more about hierarchies than about people.

"I won't argue or shout, people won't hear my voice in the streets." Those were my words in 2010 and I said them vehemently, but not too loud. But now, the world is much more chaotic than in 2010, this time we want to show a Jesus who is more straightforward, louder, and more powerful. Who puts more energy into bringing his message to the world. One of the biggest challenges for me is playing the scene at the Mount of Olives. Jesus is sweating blood and water, he feels alone, quarrels with God, and still hopes that the "cup" of death at the cross is taken from him. But in this scene, I also get very close to Jesus, because he is afraid and thus so human and not as strong as he usually is.

My fellow Jesus actor Rochus has approached the text very openly and naturally. When he acts, everything sounds very personal and feels close, I am impressed by that. I sometimes tend to slip into a somewhat holy tone on stage. I am working on that. After all, I want our audience to really feel the story. Even more, I want them to come back to the second part of the play hoping that maybe things will end differently today.

The crucifixion is strenuous, of course. First, you must drag around 90 kilos of wood. Then you hang up there at the cross, four and a half meters above the ground. You have the best view down to the audience, but all eyes are on you. Ten minutes of death agony. "Eli, eli, lama sabachtani. Into your hands, I commit my spirit." Then you die, lower your head, and breathe as shallowly as possible. I always try to empty my head completely, and show no reaction at all, almost like meditation. That's the moment when I can let go a little bit every evening. One more day of performing completed.

Then they take you off the cross, here you must play along and help a little bit. You disappear behind the stage, shower to wash off the blood, while you hear the last Halleluja out in the theatre.

Abendmahlskelch und Dornenkrone: zwei wichtige Requisiten der Passion.

The cup of the last supper and the crown of thorns: two important props of the Passion Play.

Themen sind ja auch im Passionsspiel, Jesus spricht ja genau davon. Der Text liest sich übrigens auch wie eine harte Kritik am Papst und an der Kirche, in der es zu sehr um die Hierarchien geht und weniger um die Menschen.

„Ich werde nicht streiten noch schreien, man wird meine Stimme nicht hören auf den Gassen", das sagte ich 2010 bestimmt, aber nicht zu laut. Souverän. Die Welt ist heute aber chaotischer als 2010, wir wollen diesmal einen Jesus, der zupackender, lauter ist, der Kraft in die Dinge gibt. Der mit mehr Nachdruck seine Botschaft in die Welt bringt.

Eine Herausforderung ist für mich immer die Szene am Ölberg. Jesus schwitzt Blut und Wasser, fühlt sich allein, hadert mit Gott und hofft noch, dass der Kelch an ihm vorübergeht. In der Szene komme ich ihm aber sehr nahe, weil er sich so menschlich zeigt in seiner Angst, wo er sonst so stark ist.

Mein Jesus-Kollege Rochus ist ganz frisch und unbefangen an den Text rangegangen. Bei ihm klingt alles sehr persönlich und nah, das imponiert mir. Ich habe wohl eine Tendenz, beim Spielen manchmal in einen heiligen Ton zu verfallen. Daran arbeite ich. Schließlich habe ich den Wunsch, dass die Leute wirklich mit der Geschichte mitgehen, nein, ich wünsch mir sogar, dass sie in den zweiten Teil der Vorstellung gehen und hoffen, dass es vielleicht doch anders ausgeht.

Natürlich ist auch die Kreuzigung anstrengend. Das sind 90 Kilo Holz, die du erst mal schleppen musst. Und dann hängst du da, am Kreuz, viereinhalb Meter hoch. Beste Aussicht in den Zuschauerraum, aber alle Konzentration liegt auf dir. Zehn Minuten Todeskampf, „Eli, Eli, lama sabachtani. In deine Hände lege ich meinen Geist." Dann stirbst du, senkst den Kopf, gibst dir Mühe, flach zu atmen. Ich versuche immer, den Kopf wirklich leer machen, nicht zu reagieren, einen meditativen Zustand zu erreichen. Das ist der Moment, in dem ich jedes Mal etwas loslassen kann. Wieder einen Spieltag hingekriegt.

Dann nehmen sie dich vom Kreuz, da musst du noch mal bisschen mithelfen, du verschwindest hinter der Bühne, duschst das ganze Blut ab, während draußen das letzte Halleluja erklingt.

Rochus Rückel in der Hitze Israels, September 2019.

Rochus Rückel in the heat of Israel, September 2019.

Rochus Rückel on Jesus and what it's like to play him

As a child, Jesus was the man on the donkey to me. He wasn't a Jew, but he was the boss of my religion. He was supernatural, separated from the world, although I didn't really understand what he actually did. Today, I see him as a normal human being who is unusually straightforward and unwavering. He never chooses the path of least resistance when he is faced with his opponents. And he sometimes gets angry and loud, like when he throws the moneylenders out of the temple.

My father is the organist in our church, so as a child, I was often there with him, and I had a special place next to him on the organ bench. I was always waiting for his sign for me to turn the page. I would say that I am religious, although I don't go to church regularly anymore. For me, it's not important, what you believe in. It's important that you believe in something. During our trip to Israel, we met a Holocaust survivor. He said, he would really like to believe in something, but he couldn't do so anymore. That really touched me.

When the Passion Play was canceled in 2020, I was frustrated. But, this pause of two years came at the right time for me. I finished my studies and got a master's degree in automotive engineering. Also, I was working a lot on different vehicles, I fixed a moped and a small tractor. My brother and I completely dismantled an old Unimog and then reassembled it piece by piece. Actually, I don't need all these vehicles at all, I just enjoy fixing them. Solving technical problems is like meditation for me.

In 2010, I was 14 years old and mainly just fooling around with the other kids during the Passion Play. Back then, it didn't interest me, who Jesus was but who played him. They must be really, really good, I thought. I would have never dreamed of sharing this part with Frederik,

Rochus Rückel
über Jesus und wie man den eigentlich spielt

Jesus war für mich als Kind der Mann auf dem Esel. Kein Jude, sondern der Chef meiner Religion. Er schwebte über der Menschheit, abgetrennt von allen, ohne dass ich verstanden hätte, was er eigentlich macht. Heute sehe ich in ihm einen normalen Menschen. Nur eben einen unglaublich konsequenten. Einen, der auf Gegner stößt und trotzdem nicht den Weg des geringsten Widerstands geht. Einen, der auch wütend ist, aufgebracht, wenn er die Händler aus dem Tempel scheucht.

Mein Vater ist Organist, so war ich als Kind sehr oft in der Kirche und hatte einen besonderen Platz neben ihm auf der Orgelbank. Ich wartete immer darauf, dass er mir das Zeichen zum Umblättern gab. Ich würde schon behaupten, gläubig zu sein, auch wenn ich nicht mehr jeden Sonntag in die Kirche gehe. Für mich ist es nicht wichtig, an was man glaubt. Wichtig ist, dass man glaubt. Bei unserer Reise nach Israel trafen wir uns mit einem Holocaust-Überlebenden, der sagte, er würde gern glauben, könne aber nicht mehr. Das hat mich sehr berührt.

Die Absage der Spiele 2020 hat mich frustriert, aber die zwei Jahre Pause haben mich nicht an einem schlechten Punkt im Leben erwischt. Ich habe fertig studiert und meinen Master in Fahrzeugtechnik gemacht, ich habe viel gebastelt, ein Moped repariert und einen kleinen Traktor. Einen alten Unimog haben mein Bruder und ich komplett zerlegt und Stück für Stück neu zusammengesetzt. Ich brauche diese Geräte ja überhaupt nicht, es geht mir nur darum, sie wieder fit zu machen. Technische Probleme lösen, das ist meine Meditation.

Bei der letzten Passion im Jahr 2010 war ich erst 14 und machte mit den anderen Kindern vor allem Quatsch. Damals war nicht die Person Jesus interessant, sondern die, die ihn spielten. Die müssen richtig, richtig gut sein,

Überall im Mittelpunkt, daran muss sich Rochus Rückel erst gewöhnen.

Rochus Rückel has to get used to being the center of attention.

whom I admired so, in the last Passion Play. The evening before the roles were announced publicly, in autumn 2018, Christian Stückl asked both of us to see him and told us beforehand that he had chosen us for the role. Why me? I don't know. I guess, he must have seen some potential during all those years I performed in the summer theatre.

I definitely don't want to seem arrogant, now that I got this role, like for example stop greeting people in town in the streets. That would make me feel ashamed of myself. I am very aware of the responsibility that I have, though. Like Jesus, you are the face of the Passion Play for the whole world. That means you must do a good job. At first, I was proud of every single interview I gave. By now, I am more relaxed about it. It just gets on my nerves when journalists aren't well prepared when they meet us. Some of them ask me to pick up the cross for a funny picture. That's something I don't do, because the story that we are portraying is important for many of our viewers, they believe in it. And I want to take that seriously.

"My Jesus shouldn't be hovering over others"

I don't think that playing Jesus is presumptuous. If you are allowed to paint Jesus, it's also allowed to play him. That's the freedom of art. What's much more important, is that the viewers understand that they are watching an actor portraying a role and not the real ultimate Jesus.

The Jesus that I play is not supposed to appear supernatural with halo and all. On stage, we are all equal anyway, everyone plays his or her part. If you start making differences there, you lose Jesus as a human being. Somehow, you have to manage to create an aura that makes the audience feel why it was Jesus and not anyone else that so many people chose to follow. There are some difficult passages in the text – I have to be careful to really mean the lines when I say them: "Love your enemies, do good to those who curse you, pray for those who go after you." What kind of a sentence is that? Who can manage to do that? When someone hits me, I defend myself. What I definitely don't do is turn the other cheek.

dachte ich. Ich hätte mir nicht träumen lassen, dass ich mir die Rolle bei der nächsten Passion mit dem Frederik teile, einem Jesus, den ich damals so bewundert habe. Am Abend vor der Spielerverkündung, im Herbst 2018, hat mich Spielleiter Christian Stückl zusammen mit Frederik einbestellt und uns schon verraten, dass er uns ausgewählt hat. Warum ich? Tja, eigentlich weiß ich das gar nicht. Vermutlich habe ich mich bewährt in all den Jahren beim Sommertheater.

Ich will auf keinen Fall wegen der Rolle arrogant wirken, jemanden im Dorf nicht grüßen oder so. Da würde ich mich vor mir selbst schämen. Ich hab schon Respekt vor der Verantwortung. Man vertritt als Jesus immer auch das Dorf nach draußen in die Welt. Da gilt es, ordentlich abzuliefern. Anfangs war ich stolz auf jedes Interview, inzwischen sehe ich das gelassen, bin nur genervt, wenn Journalisten sich nicht richtig informieren, bevor sie uns treffen. Manche wollen, dass man kurz mal das Kreuz nimmt für ein lustiges Foto, das mache ich nicht, denn das, was wir spielen, bedeutet manchen Zuschauern wirklich was, die glauben an die Geschichte. Ich will das ernst nehmen.

„Mein Jesus soll nicht über anderen schweben"

Ich glaube nicht, dass es anmaßend ist, Jesus zu spielen. Wenn man Jesus malen darf, darf man ihn auch spielen. Das ist die Freiheit der Kunst. Viel wichtiger ist doch, dass sich der Betrachter im Klaren ist, dass es nur eine Darstellung ist und nicht der ultimative, echte Jesus.

Mein Jesus soll nicht über den anderen schweben, so mit Heiligenschein. Auf der Bühne sind wir doch alle gleich, jeder spielt eine Rolle. Wenn man da anfängt, zwischen Einzelnen zu unterscheiden, verliert man wieder den Menschen in Jesus. Irgendwie muss man es schaffen, eine Aura zu erzeugen, sodass die Zuschauer spüren, warum ausgerechnet diesem Jesus so viele Menschen gefolgt sind. Es gibt im Passionstext einige schwierige Stellen, ich muss aufpassen, die Sätze nicht einfach so zu sprechen, sondern wirklich auch zu meinen. „Liebe deine Feinde, tu wohl denen, die dich fluchen, bete für die, die dich verfolgen." – Was ist das für ein Satz? Wer kriegt das hin? Wenn mich einer schlägt, verteidige ich mich. Aber ich halte doch gewiss nicht die andere Wange hin.

Eva-Maria Reiser
*1984 | Maria | *Mary*

How did your family react when they heard that you would play the role of Mary?
My grandma freaked out completely when she heard. We had never had the role of Mary in our family before. If everything had gone according to plan, she would have seen me play in 2020, but unfortunately, she has passed away in the meantime.

What helps you play the role?
Having to let go has been a very important thing for me over the last few years. In 2019, I could accompany my father as he passed away. And I feel that this experience makes it easier for me to understand the role of Mary. She also had to let go of someone very close to her. When I read the lines and rehearse them, I get overwhelmed by my feelings sometimes. But I also think that sometimes you have to go right where it hurts. Then something can grow from there. Initially, playing Mary was a little bit like therapy for me.

What do you do in real life?
I am a flight attendant and have been working for Lufthansa City-Line all around Europe for 15 years. Sometimes you start in Munich in the morning and wake up in Marseille the next day. Then you have French croissants for breakfast in a nice Café. For me, this job is a little bit like theatre, too. The uniform is my costume and it's a role that I play.

How is your life different now than in 2010?
In 2010 I played Mary Magdalene. And I would have played that role again, even though I was secretly hoping to get the role of Mary.

Have you ever thought about moving away from Oberammergau?
The Passion Play keeps people here. Me too. It also dictates my life, although it only happens every ten years. I do have a small apartment in Munich, but my home is here in Oberammergau. Others have beautiful mountains and meadows, too. But we have the Passion Play.

Wie hat Ihre Familie reagiert, als klar war: Sie spielen Maria?
Meine Oma ist total ausgeflippt, als sie das hörte, denn das gab's noch nie in der Familie. Wenn alles wie geplant geklappt hätte, hätte sie mich 2020 spielen sehen, leider lebt sie nun nicht mehr.

Was hilft Ihnen, die Rolle zu spielen?
Das Thema Loslassen beschäftigte mich sehr in den letzten Jahren. Ich konnte auch meinen Vater 2019 beim Sterben begleiten. Ich spüre, dass mir das die Rolle der Maria etwas greifbarer macht. Nämlich darin, jemanden loslassen zu müssen, der einem sehr nahesteht. Wenn ich die Texte lese und probe, kommt das immer mal hoch. Aber ich glaube, manchmal muss man dahin, wo es wehtut. Daraus kann was entstehen. Die Maria zu spielen war am Anfang für mich ein bisschen wie Therapie.

Was machen Sie im anderen Leben?
Ich bin Flugbegleiterin und fliege seit 15 Jahren die Lufthansa City-Line überall nach Europa. Es kann sein, dass man morgens in München startet und am nächsten Tag in Marseille aufwacht und im Café Croissants frühstückt. Der Beruf ist für mich auch ein bisschen wie Theater: Die Uniform ist das Kostüm und es ist eine Rolle, die ich da spiele.

Wie ist Ihr Leben heute anders als 2010?
2010 habe ich Maria Magdalena gespielt. Die hätte ich auch noch mal gespielt, auch wenn ich natürlich insgeheim auf die Maria gehofft hatte.

Haben Sie je überlegt, wegzuziehen aus Oberammergau?
Die Passion hält die Leute hier. Mich auch. Sie bestimmt auch mein Leben, obwohl sie nur alle zehn Jahre stattfindet. Ich habe zwar eine kleine Wohnung in München, aber mein Zuhause ist hier in Oberammergau. Schöne Berge und Wiesen haben andere auch. Aber wir haben die Passion.

Die Reise der 37 Apostel

The Journey of the 37 Apostles

Where can you get close to Jesus if not here, in Israel? For one week the actors of the Oberammergau Passion Play and their tireless director are travelling the country.

Christian Stückl auf dem Ölberg, rauchend.

Christian Stückl on the Mount of Olives, smoking.

When Christian Stückl tries to explain the Oberammergau Passion Play to an Israeli border official, he realizes how special this Play really is. It's the day of departure from Israel, a Sunday, and very early in the morning at the airport Ben Gurion in Tel Aviv. Sleepy Bavarians are sprawling on and around their suitcases. I beg your pardon? This bunch of bearded people is supposed to be a theatre group from a Bavarian village? And they are re-enacting the story of Jesus? That must be a joke – the border official is appalled – very implausible. Only after the Israeli tour guide rushes over and confirms, she accepts the story. He himself needed some time to digest it.

In September 2019, 37 Bavarians from Oberammergau go on an 8-day pilgrimage through Israel to prepare for the Passion Play. At the time, tourist groups from Australia and the USA have already bought their tickets, the performances are nearly sold out. For months the actors have let their hair grow, their beards too – the Play is scheduled to start in May 2020. Back then Corona was no more than a beer brand.

On day 5 of the trip, after the travelers have already hiked through a desert valley in burning heat, have crossed the lake Galilee by boat, and have enjoyed dozens of falafels, they reach the Garden of Gethsemane. A few feet over, some people are hugging the olive trees, overwhelmed by their religious feelings, others are sobbing. Supposedly it was right here that Judas betrayed Jesus with a kiss. If the passion of Jesus was a theatre play, this is its dramatic turning point. Cengiz Görur, just called "Cengo" by everyone, admits: "Actually, I don't really know the story that well." Sure, he heard about it at school, he says, but what exactly the Gospel of Matthew says? He would have to look it up once again. And he will surely get the chance to do so, because Cengiz Görur plays the part of Judas. Once the cast list was published in fall 2018, his name was all over the place. A Muslim playing the part of Judas who betrayed Jesus? Press reactions were divided, was this modern or rather really mean? Cengiz Görür, however, always enviably cheerful, is really relaxed about this – Muslims or Christians, that doesn't really matter, does it? When the group reaches the alleged place of Jesus' baptism, he is the first to boisterously dribble some of the muddy water over his head. Stückl is convinced that he can play the part, and that's the most important thing. The biblical stuff will come later.

Christian Stückl often tells the story, how he, when the next Passion Play is around the corner, wanders the

Unterwegs in sengender Hitze: die Gruppe auf der Festung Masada (S. 40/41) und am See Genezareth (rechts).

Walking in scorching heat: the group on the fortress of Masada (p. 40/41) and at the Sea of Galilee (right).

Wo kann man Jesus nahekommen, wenn nicht hier, in Israel? Eine Woche lang sind die Oberammergauer Passionsspieler und ihr nimmermüder Spielleiter im Land unterwegs.

Wie ungewöhnlich die Oberammergauer Passionsspiele wirklich sind, bemerkt Christian Stückl allerspätestens, als er versucht, sie einer israelischen Grenzbeamtin zu erklären. Es ist Abreisetag aus Israel, ein Sonntag, mehr Nacht als Morgen am Flughafen Ben Gurion in Tel Aviv. Schläfrige Oberammergauer lümmeln an und auf ihren Koffern. Wie bitte? Dieser bärtige Haufen soll eine Theatergruppe aus einem bayerischen Dorf sein? Eine, die die Jesus-Geschichte spielt? Das sei doch ein Witz, empört sich die Grenzbeamtin, sehr unglaubwürdig. Erst der herbeieilende israelische Reiseleiter kann vermitteln. Er hat selbst eine Weile gebraucht, bis er verstanden hat.

Im September 2019 pilgern 37 Oberammergauer acht Tage lang durch Israel, um sich auf die Passionsspiele vorzubereiten. Zu dem Zeitpunkt haben sich bereits Reisegruppen aus Australien und den USA angemeldet, die Tickets sind fast schon ausverkauft. Seit Monaten lassen sich die Darsteller die Haare wachsen, die Männer auch die Bärte, im Mai 2020 soll es losgehen. Corona war zu diesem Zeitpunkt nicht mehr als eine Biermarke.

Am fünften Tag der Reise, und da ist schon ein Wüstental bei sengender Hitze durchwandert, der See Genezareth überquert, auch etliche Falafeln sind verspeist, kommt die Gruppe im Garten Gethsemane an. Ein paar Meter weiter umarmen ein paar religiös Bewegte die Olivenbäume, manche schluchzen. Genau hier soll es gewesen sein, dass Judas Jesus durch einen Kuss verriet. Wenn die Passion ein Theaterstück ist, ist dieser Verrat sein dramatischer Wendepunkt. Cengiz Görür, den alle „Cengo" nennen, zu der Zeit 19 Jahre alt, sagt: „Ehrlich gesagt kenne ich diese Geschichte kaum." Klar, in der Schule habe er mal davon gehört, aber was nun bei Matthäus in der Bibel genau steht? Müsste er sich noch mal anschauen. Dazu wird er noch Gelegenheit haben, denn Cengiz Görür spielt den Judas. Sein Name tauchte sofort überall auf, als die Besetzung im Herbst 2018 bekannt gegeben wurde. Ein Muslim in der Rolle des Verräters Judas? Die Presse war uneinig, ob das nun supermodern oder doch eher super fies sei. Cengiz Görür aber, stets beneidenswert guter Laune, sieht das alles nicht so eng, Muslime oder Christen, ist doch irgendwie egal. Er ist der Erste, der sich beim Halt an Jesus' angeblicher Taufstelle übermütig das trübe Wasser des Jordans auf den Kopf träufelt. Stückl traut ihm die Rolle zu, das ist das Wichtigste. Das Biblische kommt schon noch.

Christian Stückl erzählt oft, wie er, wenn sich die Passion wieder ankündigt, monatelang mit „Casting-

Der Blick vom Ölberg in Jerusalem Richtung Altstadt.

The view from the Mount of Olives down to the historic centre of Jerusalem.

streets of Oberammergau scanning all passers-by for fitting parts. His casting is pure intuition. He doesn't require any of his players to be well versed in the Bible or even to be a member of the Catholic church or any other religious community. But he alone decides who plays what part. Stückl, the Jesus-Creator.

"You look like Jesus", some Americans call out to Frederik Mayet

In a passion play, however, it's obviously the part of Jesus that causes the biggest hype. This time, he is played by Frederik Mayet and Rochus Rückel, who studies automotive engineering. For Frederik Mayet, who works as press officer of the Passion Play Theatre and the Volkstheater in Munich in real life, this is the second nomination – he also played Jesus in 2010. Mayet, born in 1980, has dark blond hair, an impressive beard and a friendly face.

Phenotypically, he is just the kind of Jesus that Germans have in mind – and Americans, too, apparently.

In the streets of Jerusalem, two American tourists stop him and call out enthusiastically: "You look like Jesus!" Even back in 2010, says Mayet, some emotionally overwhelmed viewers came to him after the play and celebrated him as the chosen one. And there is nothing he can do about that. Whoever plays Jesus in the Passion Play, is often taken for the real Jesus. As inconceivable this biblical story is, many believers, it seems, are longing for something – or someone – they can see and touch. That was something Frederik Mayet had to learn first. And Rochus Rückel will have to learn it too. He was born in 1996, which makes him the second youngest Jesus in the history of the Passion Play.

Each one of the 37 travelers brings his or her own story to Israel. Among them are innkeepers, sculptors, students, architects, pupils, hotel owners, caterers, foresters, and one of the two Marys is a flight attendant. They all adjust their work schedules to be part of the play, some of them even move back to Oberammergau as all actors must have their main residence here. Ursula Mayr who plays Veronica, comments: "Every ten years our

David Bender, Sebastian Dörfler und Frederik Mayet in Caesarea (oben, von links nach rechts). Ein Minenfeld nahe der Taufstelle Jesu am Jordan erinnert an den Nahostkonflikt (unten).

David Bender, Sebastian Dörfler and Frederik Mayet in Caesarea (above, from left to right). A minefield near the place of Jesus' baptism at the river Jordan – a reminder of the Middle East conflict (below).

blick" durch die Straßen Oberammergaus schleicht und die Menschen auf passende Rollen prüft. Er besetze nur intuitiv. Bibelfestigkeit, die Mitgliedschaft in der katholischen Kirche oder irgendeinen religiösen Glauben setzt er nicht voraus. Aber er allein entscheidet, wer welche Rolle spielt. Stückl, der Jesusmacher.

„You look like Jesus", rufen ein paar Amerikaner Frederik Mayet zu

Naturgemäß ist bei einem Passionsspiel der Hype um den Jesus am größten. Diesmal spielen ihn Frederik Mayet und Rochus Rückel, Student der Fahrzeugtechnik. Für Frederik Mayet, der im normalen Leben Pressesprecher des Passions- und des Münchner Volkstheaters ist, ist dies schon die zweite Ernennung, schon 2010 war er Jesus. Mayet, Jahrgang 1980, hat dunkelblondes Haar, einen stattlichen Bart und ein freundliches Gesicht. Phänotypisch ziemlich genau eine Art Jesus, wie man ihn sich hierzulande gern vorstellt. Offenbar auch in den USA: Auf der Straße in Jerusalem stoppen ihn zwei amerikanische Touristen. „You look like Jesus!", rufen sie begeistert. Schon 2010, erzählt Mayet, suchten ihn nach der Vorstellung in Oberammergau ein paar emotional Überwältigte auf und feierten ihn als Auserwählten. Wehren konnte er sich kaum. Wer bei der Passion den Jesus spielt, wird auch gern mal für Jesus gehalten. Bei aller Unfassbarkeit dieser biblischen Geschichte sehnen sich die Gläubigen offenbar nach etwas, das sie sehen und berühren können. Beziehungsweise nach jemandem. Das musste Frederik Mayet erst lernen. Und das wird Rochus Rückel lernen müssen, geboren 1996 und somit der zweitjüngste Jesus der Passionsspielgeschichte.

Jeder der 37 bringt eine andere Geschichte mit nach Israel. Unter ihnen sind Gastwirte, Bildhauerinnen, Studierende, Architektinnen, Schüler, Hoteliers, Caterer, Förster, eine der beiden Marias ist Flugbegleiterin. Um bei der Passion mitspielen zu können, passen sie

DIE REISE DER 37 APOSTEL

Abkühlung bei großer Hitze im Toten Meer (rechts).
Veronika-Darstellerin Veronika Hecht (unten).

*The Dead Sea offers a bit of refreshment in the
extreme heat (right). Veronika Hecht who plays the role
of Veronica (below).*

town changes; for a few months life here is different, everyday routines are on hold. Others must move for events like this one, we don't even have to leave Oberammergau." The youngest actor is 16 at the time of the trip, the oldest is 78 years old. This is Peter Stückl, Passion Play veteran and father of the director. He first took part in the play in 1950, an immeasurably long time ago. Back then, the actor of Jesus had to be a pietistic Adonis, married women were not allowed to play the part of Mary, and hardly anybody cared about antisemitic passages in the text.

The family trees of some of the actors read like a VIP list of the Passion Play. Let's take the Preisinger family for example – there is always a family member called Anton, and remarkably often the actor of Jesus is called Preisinger by last name. This year Anton IV and Anton V are part of the play as Pilatus and the disciple John. Then there is the Huber family, which has fewer leading roles to pride itself with, but nevertheless countless family members on stage over the years – this year it's Ursula playing Veronica. Then there is Maxi Stöger – not to be confused with his brother Christoph Stöger, who is also part of the travel group. Maximilian Stöger, born in 1988 and a forestry engineer by profession, used to be the head altar boy. "Why does Jesus need miracles?" he asks his fellow travelers during an excursion on the Sea of Galilee, while the water is gently rocking the boat. Good question. It is sweltering hot and so windless that the group can hear the singing of the pilgrims on the neighboring boat. "Isn't a miracle a rather crude demonstration of his supernaturalism?" asks Stöger. He would surely be a good Jesus, too, but he plays Caiaphas, the Jewish high priest who, according to the Bible, was part of the condemnation of Jesus. It's one of the most important parts in the play and should not be underestimated.

*During a prayer the voice of
a Muezzin flies into the room*

He and the group get some answers from Thomas Frauenlob, priest and theological guide this week. From his New Testament, held together by a red rubber band, he tirelessly reads the appropriate passages, while the group tries to escape the heat in the shadow of ficus trees and church walls. Matthew, Chapter 14: Jesus walks on the

Arbeitsverträge an, manche ziehen nach Oberammergau zurück, weil nur spielberechtigt ist, wer dort den Hauptwohnsitz hat. Veronika-Darstellerin Ursula Mayr beschreibt es so: „Alle zehn Jahre verändert sich was im Ort, das Leben funktioniert ein paar Monate anders, der Alltag wird unterbrochen. Andere müssen für so was umziehen, wir müssen Oberammergau nicht mal verlassen." Der jüngste Spieler ist zur Zeit der Reise 16, der älteste ist 78 Jahre alt, es ist Peter Stückl, Passions-Veteran und Spielleiter-Vater. 1950 war er zum ersten Mal dabei, unendlich lang ist das her, da musste der Jesus noch ein frömmelnder Schönling sein, verheiratete Frauen durften nicht die Maria spielen und so ziemlich niemand störte sich an antisemitischen Passagen im Text.

Die Familienstammbäume mancher Spieler lesen sich wie eine VIP-Liste der Passion. Da ist die Preisinger-Dynastie zum Beispiel, in der immer einer Anton heißt und die auffällig oft den Jesus hervorbrachte. Anton IV. und Anton V. sind diesmal dabei, als Pilatus und Jünger Johannes. Dann die Huber-Dynastie, die zwar mit weniger Hauptrollen, dafür aber mit umfassenderem Familieneinsatz punkten kann, diesmal vertreten durch Veronika-Darstellerin Ursula. Dann gibt es den Stöger-Maxi, nicht zu verwechseln mit seinem ebenfalls mitgereisten Bruder, dem Stöger-Christoph. Maximilian Stöger, Jahrgang 1988, Forstingenieur, war mal Oberministrant. „Warum brauchte Jesus Wunder?", fragt er in die Runde bei einer Schifffahrt auf dem See Genezareth, das Wasser gluckst behäbig an das Boot. Gute Frage. Es ist drückend heiß und so windstill, dass man vom Nachbarboot die Pilgergesänge hören kann. „Ist ein Wunder nicht eine eher plumpe Demonstration seiner Übermenschlichkeit?", fragt Stöger. Er gäbe sicher auch einen feinen Jesus ab, spielt aber Kaiphas, den jüdischen Hohepriester, der laut Bibel an Jesus' Verurteilung beteiligt gewesen sein soll. Eine der wichtigsten Rollen der Passion, nicht zu unterschätzen.

Bei einer Andacht fliegt von draußen die Stimme eines Muezzin herein

Ein paar Antworten bekommen er und die Gruppe von Thomas Frauenlob, Priester und theologischer Begleiter in dieser Woche. Aus seinem Neuen Testament, zusam-

DIE REISE DER 37 APOSTEL

Waren die Jünger ein lahmer Haufen, oder fand man die sympathisch? Waren Frauen dabei? Andrea Hecht (Maria) diskutiert.

Were the disciples a bunch of bores, or did people like them? Were there women among them? Andrea Hecht (Mary) in discussion.

water at the Sea of Galilee; Matthew, Chapter 26: Jesus asks his disciples to be watchful in the Garden of Gethsemane. Frauenlob doesn't only have the right Bible verse at hand, but also a couple of jokes on women and some good arguments for celibacy. When the sounds of the Muezzin fly into the room during a prayer in St. Anna in Jerusalem, he has the church door closed. This moment reveals so much about Jerusalem and its people: they gather to pray, here and there, and the borders between religions are blurred. Before God, the Bible says, they are all equal anyway.

Perhaps Jesus didn't always speak wisely and unctuously, perhaps he was angry and upset sometimes.

Christian Stückl is critical of the church, and he already invited Frauenlob to be part of his travel group to Israel ten years ago. One reason might be the greatly intense arguments he can have with him. There is no mistaking, however, who has the final word. "Later, we'll sit down and chat for a while," Stückl says, still not tired after a twelve-hour day program. A phrase, often quoted by his people. Stückl seems to have no physical needs, apart from his cigarettes. He smokes almost incessantly as if it were the cigarettes that could give him all the energy he needs. Even in the most unbearable heat, he wears – as usual – long jeans, a shirt, and his typical bavarian "Haferl shoes" – which as a principle he never ties. He has more important things to do.

Christian Stückl is open to spirituality and religion, although he explicitly does not call himself religious, let alone catholic. "The texts of the Bible, its values have always inspired me," he says. For him, the passion of Jesus is much more than a theatre play, and yet he has no problem asking practical questions as any other play

mengehalten durch ein rotes Gummiband, liest er unermüdlich die passenden Stellen vor, während die Gruppe der Hitze auch im Schatten von Ficusbäumen und Kirchenmauern kaum entkommt. Matthäus, Kapitel 14: Jesus geht über das Wasser am See Genezareth, Matthäus, Kapitel 26: Jesus fordert seine Jünger zur Wachsamkeit auf im Garten Gethsemane. Frauenlob hat neben der richtigen Bibelstelle auch einige Frauenwitze sowie gute Argumente für den Zölibat parat. Als bei einer Andacht in St. Anna in Jerusalem von draußen die Klänge des Muezzin hereinschweben, lässt er die Kirchentüren schließen. Ein Moment, der doch so viel über Jerusalem und die Menschen erzählt: Man versammelt sich zum Gebet, hier wie dort, die Grenzen verschwimmen. Vor Gott, das steht auch in der Bibel, sind doch sowieso alle gleich.

Vielleicht hat Jesus ja nicht nur salbungsvoll geredet, sondern war wütend, aufgebracht.

Der kirchenkritische Christian Stückl hat Frauenlob schon bei der letzten Reise nach Israel vor zehn Jahren mitgenommen. Vielleicht auch, weil er so herrlich mit ihm streiten kann. Wer das letzte Wort hat, steht ohnehin außer Frage. „Nachher ratsch mer noch ein bisserl", sagt Stückl, wenn er nach einem Zwölf-Stunden-Tagesprogramm noch immer nicht müde ist. Ein Satz, den seine Leute oft zitieren werden. Stückl scheint kein körperliches Bedürfnis zu kennen, abgesehen von dem nach den Zigaretten, die er beinahe pausenlos aussaugt, so, als gäben sie ihm alle nötige Energie. Auch in unerträglicher Hitze trägt er, wie eigentlich immer, lange Jeans, Hemd und Haferlschuhe. Diese übrigens schnürt er grundsätzlich nicht. Er hat Wichtigeres zu tun.

Für Spiritualität und Religion ist Christian Stückl offen, auch wenn er sich nicht explizit als gläubig oder gar katholisch bezeichnet. „Mich begeistern die Texte der Bibel immer schon, die Werte", sagt er. Die Passionsgeschichte geht für ihn weit über einen Theatertext hinaus, trotzdem hat er kein Problem, als Regisseur ganz praktische Fragen an den Text zu stellen: Wie roch es damals? Wie sah es auf den Straßen aus? Wie war die Stimmung im römisch besetzten Judäa, in das Jesus hineinwirkte? Waren die Jünger ein lahmer Haufen, oder fand man die sympathisch? Waren Frauen dabei? Stückl nimmt jedes Wort des Neuen Testaments erst mal ernst, prüft, dreht es, als könne er noch etwas finden, das ihm bislang entgangen ist.

Vielleicht habe Jesus nicht nur salbungsvoll dahergeredet, sondern war wütend, kämpferisch? „Selig, die arm sind vor Gott? Damit meint er doch: Gschissen auf die Reichen!" Und wie muss man sich eigentlich diesen Tod am Kreuz vorstellen? „Was hat er denn wirklich gesagt am Kreuz? Was sagt man überhaupt so am Kreuz?", überlegt Stückl an der Grabeskirche in Jerusalem. Die Gruppe lehnt wieder mal im Schatten, nachdem sie die Via Dolorosa entlanggegangen ist, den Leidens-

Hat immer einen (Bibel-)Spruch parat: Theologe Thomas Frauenlob.

Theologian Thomas Frauenlob always has the appropriate (biblical) saying on his lips.

director would do: What did it smell like back then? What did the streets look like? How was life for the people in Judea, which was occupied by the Romans? Were the disciples a bunch of bores or did people like them? Were there women among them? Stückl begins by taking every word from The New Testament seriously, examining it and turning it in his head as if looking for something he has missed so far.

Perhaps Jesus didn't always speak wisely and unctuously, but was angry and fierce sometimes? "Blessed are the poor before God? Didn't he really mean: Screw all the rich people!" And how should we imagine his death on the cross? "What did he really say on the cross? What would one say hanging on a cross?" Stückl ponders standing at the Church of the Holy Sepulcher in Jerusalem. Once again, the group is leaning in the shade after having walked down the Via Dolorosa, Jesus' way of suffering, where dozens of pilgrim groups carry down their wooden crosses these days.

His next Jesus won't be nice and sweet, Stückl knows that. During this week in Israel the play production machine in his head begins to form the image of a social revolutionary. A man who is driven, demanding, obsessed maybe. A man who loudly expresses his outrage about the gaps between the rich and the poor. The question that always tortures Stückl is, how to put all this on stage without it seeming ridiculous, theatrical, blasphemous, presumptuous, pietistic, or awkwardly catholic.

Jesus shouldn't be too modern either; every now and again, Stückl gets in trouble with some – albeit few – opponents he has in town. Shortly before the group left for Israel, the local council rejected a public petition initiated to prevent the planned renovation of the stage. And others get involved, too: The animal welfare organization Peta recently demanded that Jesus shouldn't ride into the Passion Play Theatre on a real donkey. Instead, why not choose an E-Scooter for his entrance? Thus, PR-Jesus Frederik Mayet, standing on the roof of the Church of the Holy Sepulcher, has to explain to journalists via mobile phone that the donkey is perfectly fine and that there are no plans to switch to an E-Scooter any time soon.

One of the travelers recounts that during one performance of the Passion Play, just at the moment when they put up the cross, a violent thunderstorm began. There was lightning and loud thunder, and 17 spectators fainted. But even Oberammergau cannot always count on such heavenly support, Stückl must find and create

weg Jesu, über den heute Pilgergruppen die Holzkreuze im Akkord tragen.

Bloß nicht zu lieb soll er sein, der Jesus, das weiß Stückl schon. In der parallel laufenden Inszenierungsmaschine in seinem Kopf formt sich in der Woche das Bild eines Sozialrevolutionärs. Ein Getriebener, ein Fordernder, vielleicht ein Besessener. Einer, der sich laut über die Gräben zwischen Arm und Reich empört. Und immer quält Stückl die Frage, wie man das auf der Bühne darstellt, ohne dass es lächerlich, theatral, blasphemisch, anmaßend, frömmelnd, unangenehm katholisch wirkt.

Zu modern darf es außerdem auch nicht sein, immer mal wieder gibt es Knatsch mit Gegnern aus dem Dorf, von denen Stückl ein paar wenige, aber dennoch welche hat. Kurz vor Abreise erst wurde im Gemeinderat ein Bürgerbegehren abgeschmettert, das den geplanten Umbau der Bühne verhindern sollte. Und auch andere mischen sich ein, von der Tierschutzorganisation Peta kommt in der Woche die Forderung, Jesus möge doch bitte nicht mehr auf einem echten Esel ins Passionstheater reiten, sondern man solle über eine Einfahrt auf dem E-Scooter nachdenken. So muss Presse-Jesus Frederik Mayet vom Dach der Grabeskirche aus Journalisten per Telefon erklären, dem Esel gehe es bestens, auf einen E-Scooter oder andere Elektromobile würde man bis auf Weiteres nicht umsteigen.

Einmal, erzählt einer der Mitreisenden, sei bei der Passion ein Gewitter losgebrochen, genau in dem Moment, als sie das Kreuz aufstellten. Es donnerte laut, 17 Zuschauer wurden ohnmächtig. Auf solch himmlischen Beistand kann man sich aber selbst in Oberammergau nicht verlassen, man muss schon selbst Bilder finden. „Christian, jetzt reicht's!", ruft der alte Peter Stückl seinem Sohn öfter von der Seite zu. Es reicht nie. In dieser Woche ist es definitiv nicht Jesus, dem gefolgt wird.

Stückl will sich und seine Leute mit Eindrücken und Fragen überfordern

Manche überfordert das Nimmersatte, andere finden die Diskussionen zu theologisch. „Ich fühl mich grad noch ziemlich im Wald", sagt der zweite Jesus Rochus Rückel am Ende der Reise. Ein paar mehr Pausen wären schön, einfach mal im lauschigen Garten des Pilgerhauses sitzen, in dem die Gruppe wohnt. Doch das eng getaktete Programm lässt oft nicht mal Zeit, in Ruhe aufzuessen.

Die Reise führt nach Nazareth in die Verkündigungskirche, in die Straßen von Jerusalem, zum Gespräch mit dem Holocaust-Überlebenden Abba Naor (links von oben) und nach Yad Vashem (oben).

The journey leads to the Church of the Annunciation in Nazareth, into the streets of Jerusalem, to a discussion with Holocaust survivor Abba Naor (left top down) as well as to Yad Vashem (above).

powerful images himself. "Christian, enough!", the old Peter Stückl often calls out to his son. It is never enough. During this week in Israel, it is not Jesus who is being followed.

Stückl wants to challenge and overwhelm his crew and himself with impressions and questions

Some of them are overwhelmed by his insatiable energy, others think the discussions are too theological. "I still feel confused and quite lost," says the second Jesus, Rochus Rückel, at the end of the trip. A few more breaks would have been nice, just sitting in the cozy, secluded garden of their pilgrim's hostel for a while. The tightly scheduled program, however, often doesn't even give them enough time to finish their meals. A visit to Jerusalem alone is challenging and strenuous. All over the city, heavily armed soldiers are a constant reminder of the latent conflicts in Israel. The narrow streets are always crowded with Muslims, orthodox Jews, Christians and tourists and others that are hard to classify as things here are rarely ever simple and clear. Stückl wants to overwhelm himself and his crew. He is convinced that you must first feel really lost in the woods before you can start to work your way out.

Part of this overwhelming experience is a visit to the Holocaust Memorial Yad Vashem and a discussion with Holocaust survivor Abba Naor who welcomes the group in the stuffy conference room of a hotel in Tel Aviv. The Passion Play has had its inglorious times, too. Adolf Hitler declared them "important for the Deutsche Reich". And for centuries antisemitic resentments were shown unreflected and thoughtless on stage.

Stückl has been in close contact with Jews and rabbis for years about this subject; he is very serious about banning any obvious or hidden antisemitism from the Passion Play. Abba Naor, born in 1928, has survived the concentration camp and a death march in Bavaria, he speaks to the group free from anger and resentment: "Life is a great thing, isn't it?" Another sentence frequently quoted by the trip members.

Stückl has been in close contact with rabbis and theologians for years

Incidentally, a small miracle happens on the trip: they all turn into a close group. One sign of this is the lack of seating arrangements in busses and dining rooms. Once you have stammered Hebrew songs at the Wailing wall together, hiked through hot desert valleys and paddled in the Dead Sea, you are connected in a special way. Growing hair and beards may be an external sign of connection, but it's the sweat that makes them all a team.

"Has the trip helped you at all?", Stückl asks on the last day – and he also asks himself the question. He, too, is still a bit lost. Now he faces the enormous task of turning all of this into a story that is convincing and touching, no matter if a viewer is religious or not. First, he plans to finish writing the text at home. Rehearsals will start in December 2019. He is still far from being done.

In der Grabeskirche in Jerusalem betet eine Pilgerin am sogenannten Salbungsstein.

In the Church of the Holy Sepulcher in Jerusalem a pilgrim is praying at the so-called Stone of Anointing.

Jerusalem allein ringt seinen Besuchern ja schon einiges ab. Die Stadt, in der die überall präsenten, schwerst bewaffneten Soldaten jederzeit an die Konflikte Israels erinnern. Wo man im Gewusel der engen Gassen Muslimen und orthodoxen Juden begegnet, Christen und Touristen, und solchen, die man nirgends zuordnen kann, weil die Dinge ja nun mal oft nicht eindeutig sind. Stückl will sich und seine Leute überfordern. Er glaubt, dass man erst sehr tief in den Wald rein muss, um dann raus zu finden.

Dazu gehört auch der Besuch der Holocaust-Gedenkstätte Yad Vashem und ein Gespräch mit dem Holocaust-Überlebenden Abba Naor, der die Gruppe im stickigen Tagungsraum eines Hotels in Tel Aviv empfängt. Die Passionsspiele haben auch unrühmliche Momente erlebt, Adolf Hitler erklärte die Spiele einst für „reichswichtig", auch antisemitische Ressentiments wurden jahrhundertelang sehr unreflektiert auf der Bühne gepflegt. Stückl tauscht sich seit Jahren intensiv mit Juden und Rabbinern darüber aus, es ist ihm ernst damit, offensichtlichen oder versteckten Antisemitismus im Passionsspiel erst gar nicht mehr vorkommen zu lassen. Abba Naor, geboren 1928, hat das Konzentrationslager und einen Todesmarsch in Bayern überlebt. Er spricht frei von Groll und Wut: „Das Leben ist doch eine feine Sache." Auch diesen Satz werden die Oberammergauer oft zitieren.

Stückl tauscht sich seit Jahren mit Rabbis und Theologen über die Passion aus

Ganz nebenbei geschieht auf dieser Reise das Wunder der Gruppenwerdung. Man erkennt das zum Beispiel an der nicht vorhandenen Sitzordnung in Bus und Speisesälen. Mit wem man mal an der Klagemauer hebräische Lieder gestottert, heiße Wüstentäler durchwandert und im Toten Meer geplanscht hat, dem begegnet man danach anders. Sich Bärte und Haare wachsen zu lassen verbindet vielleicht äußerlich, der Schweiß erst tauft das Team.

„Hat's euch was gebracht?", fragt Stückl am letzten Tag der Reise, und er fragt sich das auch ein wenig selbst. Der Wald ist auch bei ihm noch da. Er steht nun vor der immensen Aufgabe, daraus eine Geschichte hervorzuholen, die überzeugt und berührt, egal ob ein Zuschauer gläubig ist oder nicht. Den Text will Stückl als Nächstes fertig schreiben, zu Hause, im Dezember 2019 werden Proben beginnen. Er ist noch lang nicht fertig.

Unverkennbar: der Felsendom mit der goldenen Kuppel.

A distinctive landmark: the Dome of the Rock with its golden cupola.

Cengiz Görür
* 2000 | Judas | *Judas*

What did you do during the two years between the cancelation and the Passion Play 2022?
In 2020 I quit school for the Passion Play, and then it was canceled. There was a huge void after that. I decided to do an apprenticeship as an automobile salesman, but soon I noticed that this wasn't what I wanted. Then, Christian Stückl, our director, asked, if I didn't want to try acting. I didn't know anything about acting at the time, so I applied to drama school – and was accepted. All the other students knew dramas, texts and plots and went to the theatre all the time – I didn't. I commuted to Munich, and was constantly on the road. After half a year I was totally exhausted and extremely unhappy. I dropped out of school. For one year I did various odd jobs, like delivering pizza. Then the directors of the drama school approached me and told me: We see your potential, if you want to try again, you can come back to school. And I have decided to do it. I'll try again in autumn.

How did it come you are part of the Passion Play?
I was sitting in an ice cream parlor in Oberammergau with my mother, when Christian Stückl addressed me from the table next to ours. He called: "Cengiz, see you in 15 minutes in the Passion Play Theatre. I want to hear your voice on stage." That was back in 2016. So I went to the theatre. And I stayed.

Is faith important to you?
I am a Muslim and have been raised in that faith. But I am very open. My faith has taught me how to approach and treat other people. We are all the same, no matter if we are Muslims, Christians, or Jews. You just have to be a good person, it's as simple as that.

Judas is a very complex character. What's it like to play him?
It's the very first time that a young Muslim plays the part of Judas. In fact, a Muslim has never had such an important role in the Passion Play. This is huge. I am really grateful. Initially, all I knew about Judas was, that he betrays Jesus. In the meantime, I have read a lot and done some research. That has helped me a lot. And the short training at drama school has also helped me to approach the role in a totally new way after the long break.

Wie haben Sie die zwei Jahre zwischen der Absage und den Spielen 2022 verbracht?
Ich habe 2020 die Schule abgebrochen für die Passion, und dann fiel die aus. Da war eine riesige Leere. Ich wollte eine Ausbildung machen, als Automobilkaufmann, aber dann fiel mir auf, dass ich da gar keine Lust drauf habe. „Willst du nicht Schauspiel probieren?", hat mich unser Spielleiter Christian Stückl gefragt. Ich wusste gar nicht, wie das geht, Schauspieler werden, also habe ich mich an der Schauspielschule beworben – und bin genommen worden. Alle anderen kannten Dramen und Texte, gingen ständig ins Theater, ich nicht. Ich bin nach München gependelt, war nur noch unterwegs, nach einem halben Jahr konnte ich nicht mehr, ich war total unglücklich. Und bin ausgestiegen. Ich habe ein Jahr lang gejobbt, Pizza ausgeliefert. Die Schulleiter der Schauspielschule haben mir damals gesagt, Cengiz, wir sehen was in dir, wenn du es noch mal probieren willst, kannst du es noch mal probieren. Und ich habe mich entschieden: Ich mach's, ich greif noch mal an im Herbst.

Wie kommt es, dass Sie bei der Passion mitspielen?
Ich saß mit meiner Mutter in einem Eiscafé in Oberammergau, als mich Christian Stückl vom Nebentisch aus rief: „Cengiz, in 15 Minuten im Passionstheater. Ich will mal deine Stimme auf der Bühne hören." Das war 2016. Also bin ich hin ins Theater. Und bin geblieben.

Spielt der Glaube eine Rolle für Sie?
Ich bin Moslem und auch so erzogen. Aber ich bin sehr offen. Der Glaube hat vor allem geprägt, wie ich mit anderen Menschen umgehe. Wir sind alle gleich, egal ob Moslem, Christ oder Jude. Man muss ein lieber Mensch sein, ganz einfach.

Judas ist eine eher komplizierte Figur. Wie ist es, ihn zu spielen?
Es war noch nie so, dass ein so junger Moslem den Judas spielte. Dass ein Moslem überhaupt so eine große Rolle in der Passion hatte. Eine riesengroße Sache. Ich bin total dankbar. Ich wusste anfangs über Judas nur, dass er Jesus verrät. Ich hab dann viel nachgelesen und recherchiert, das hat mir sehr geholfen. Durch die kleine Ausbildung an der Schauspielschule bin ich nach der langen Pause auch ganz anders ans Spielen rangegangen.

Barbara Schuster
* 1986 | Maria Magdalena | *Mary Magdalene*

Does your family have much Passion Play tradition?
Not really. My mother is from a neighboring village. By now, she would be allowed to participate in the play, but she doesn't want to. My grandparents are Sudeten Germans and came to Oberammergau after World War II. Back then, they weren't allowed to be part of the play, and they accepted that. I think, if you had to leave everything behind, flee from your home to a new country, you don't question anything there. My father, who was born here, was the only one who always participated in the play with great enthusiasm.

You play Mary Magdalene. How do you see this role?
Magdalene is one of Jesus' faithful companions and she doesn't care what people say. She wants to support him because she knows that he has a hard way ahead of him. I especially like her appearance after the entry into Jerusalem. Judas is nagging that it's time to go to war against the Romans. She counters: "Is your slavery so hard? Is your suffering so severe? God's sun is shining on the land and our vines are blossoming in peace."

Does the Passion Play need more women?
Our director has already done a lot to give women a greater significance in the play. But more is always possible, women could have more important text passages, or sources other than the Bible could be used. It's clear that the Bible isn't very feminist – there is nothing we can do about that. But having women play some of the disciples? For me, that's not an option.

Is faith important to you?
Not for my role in the Passion Play. It is not a play of faith but a play of tradition. I don't have to be Catholic for that.

What does your life look like now?
I am on parental leave at the moment. When the Passion Play was canceled in 2020, we changed our plans, and I had another baby. I am very happy with how things have gone. Normally, I work in the HR department of a bank in Munich. My husband plays Judas. Magdalene and Judas are both great fans of Jesus, but at the same time they are also opponents, they represent different ideas of Jesus. A convenient thing is that Judas commits suicide shortly after the intermission while I don't have to be back in the theatre until the way of the cross – so the babysitting problem is solved.

Gibt es bei Ihnen eine Familien-Passionstradition?
Wenig. Meine Mutter kommt aus dem Nachbardorf, die dürfte zwar mitspielen, will aber nicht. Meine Großeltern sind Sudetendeutsche und kamen nach dem Zweiten Weltkrieg nach Oberammergau. Sie durften damals nicht mitspielen, das haben sie hingenommen. Ich glaube, wenn man alles stehen und liegen lassen muss in der Heimat und in ein neues Land flüchtet, dann stellt man dort erst mal nichts infrage. Nur mein Vater, der ist hier geboren und war immer mit totaler Begeisterung dabei.

Sie spielen Maria Magdalena. Wie sehen Sie diese Rolle?
Magdalena ist eine treue Begleiterin von Jesus und gibt wenig drauf, was die Leute reden. Sie will ihn stärken, weil sie weiß, dass er einen harten Weg gehen muss. Ich mag besonders ihren Auftritt nach dem Einzug nach Jerusalem. Judas stichelt, dass es Zeit wäre, gegen die Römer in den Krieg zu ziehen. Sie setzt dem was entgegen und sagt: „Ist so hart eure Knechtschaft? Ist so brennend euer Leiden? Es ist Gottes Sonne über dem Land und unsere Weinstöcke blühen in Frieden."

Braucht die Passion mehr Frauen?
Unser Spielleiter hat schon einiges getan, die Frauenfiguren aufzuwerten. Aber da ginge schon noch was, man könnte ihnen noch mehr sinnhaltige Sätze geben, oder auch andere Quellen als die Bibel heranziehen. Denn die ist nun mal nicht sehr feministisch, da ist kaum mehr rauszuholen. Und Jünger von Frauen spielen zu lassen? Das wäre keine Option für mich.

Spielt der Glaube für Sie eine Rolle?
Zum Spielen nicht. Es ist kein Glaubensspiel, sondern ein Traditionsspiel. Ich muss dafür nicht katholisch sein.

Wie sieht Ihr Leben gerade aus?
Ich bin in Elternzeit. Als die Passionsspiele 2020 ausgefallen sind, haben wir umgeplant, ich habe ein zweites Kind bekommen. Ich bin sehr happy, dass das so gelaufen ist. Sonst arbeite ich in der Personalabteilung einer Bank in München. Mein Mann spielt Judas. Magdalena und Judas sind beide totale Fans von Jesus, aber gleichzeitig so etwas wie Kontrahenten, sie stehen für unterschiedliche Vorstellungen von Jesus. Sehr praktisch ist, dass sich Judas kurz nach der Vorstellungspause das Leben nimmt und ich erst wieder zum Kreuzweg ins Theater muss – somit ist das Babysitterproblem gelöst.

Stückls Plan und Gottes Beitrag

Stückl's Plan and God's Contribution

Wie aus den Passionsspielen 2020 die Passionspiele 2022 wurden.

Ein Making-of-Drama in 12 Szenen

How the Passion Play 2020 became the Passion Play 2022.

A Making-of-drama in 12 Scenes

In den Werkstätten des Passionstheaters beginnt die Arbeit viele Monate vor den Proben. Auch hier arbeiten fast ausschließlich Oberammergauer.

In the workshops of the theatre, work begins months before the rehearsals. Here too, the workers are mostly locals.

Scene 1:
The Beginning

Traditionally, the "Hair and Beard Decree" enters into force on Ash Wednesday of the year before the Passion Play. This is the day the men of Oberammergau are allowed to shave for the last time. After that they have more than a year to grow and cultivate substantial beards. Beards just like Jesus and his disciples might have worn. Those who don't like beards can still play a Roman – they are allowed to shave and are therefore quite popular parts. And the women who take part in the play also have time to grow their hair. From now on it's the hair that shows who is part of the Passion Play, and who isn't. The Passion Play – this world-famous staged production of the last days of Jesus, which every ten years, causes an entire Bavarian town to melt into a gigantic theatre family. This time, the "Beard Decree" falls on March 6, 2019. And that's also the day our story begins.

The other story, however, begins much earlier, nearly 400 years earlier, in 1633. When the plague raged in Europe, the people of Oberammergau turned to the Lord in all their desperation and promised him a passion play, if he just freed them from the plague. Legend says that after this promise no more people from Oberammergau died of the Black Death. So, since 1634, they have put the Passion Play on stage, in a slowed down ten-year-rhythm. Only people who are born in town or have lived there for more than twenty years are allowed to participate. So, the Jesus actors are people from Oberammergau as well as the stage designer, the tailors, the members of the choir and the orchestra, and the ticket attendants. They are students, civil servants, architects, forestry engineers, and sculptors, one of them is a flight attendant, and the man who plays Pontius Pilatus runs a hotel in town. None of them is a professional actor. It's a crazy thing, of course, that it's amateur actors of all people, who say the most pompous words on stage – but there is nothing normal about the Passion Play anyway.

The director, Christian Stückl, is a stereotype "Oberammergauer". He was born in 1961 and raised in a traditional inn. There, as a little boy, he listened to the grown-ups discussing the Passion Play. Later, he organized and rehearsed theatre plays in the dining hall when his parents were on vacation in November. Stückl, a trained woodcarver, is now the director of the "Volkstheater", a theatre in Munich. As director of the Passion Play, he must fit everyone, who wants to participate, somewhere on or behind the stage, that's what the so-called "playing rights" specify. This time, 2,100 of the total 5,400 inhabitants of Oberammergau take part in the play – most of them on, and many behind the stage. Those who have moved away, come back to town for the Passion Play. Those who live there, reorganize their lives around the play. To miss this event is unthinkable.

Letting the hair and beards grow is more than the attempt to copy biblical hairdos. Every inch of hair marks another step on their common path toward the play. They have waited for almost ten years. The last Passion Play in 2010 is a long time ago. Back then, Thomas Müller was the best junior player in the soccer world championship and Lena Meyer-Landrut won the Eurovision Song Contest. And Cengiz Görur was ten years old.

On the day of the Hair and Beard Decree, he still wears an undercut, and he constantly runs his fingers through his hair. He plays Judas. Like all the other actors he has known this since October 2018, when the roles and their actors were publicly announced in front of a large audience and curious journalists. Back then, his name was written in elegant letters on a large blackboard outside of the Passion Play Theatre. Each of the 21 main

Oberammergauerinnen schauen nach, wer welche Rolle bei der Passion spielen wird.

Girls from Oberammergau check who will play which part in the Passion Play.

Im Herbst 2018 findet vor dem Theater die Spielerverkündung statt.

The announcement of the parts takes place in fall 2018 in front of the theatre.

Szene 1:
Der Anfang

Der „Haar- und Barterlass" tritt traditionell am Aschermittwoch des Jahres vor der Passion in Kraft. Das ist der Tag, an dem sich die Männer in Oberammergau zum letzten Mal rasieren dürfen. Mehr als ein Jahr haben sie dann Zeit, sich ernstzunehmende Bärte zu kultivieren. Bärte, wie Jesus und seine Jünger sie vielleicht trugen. Wer gar keine Lust hat auf einen Bart, spielt halt einen Römer, denn die dürfen sich rasieren und gehören deshalb durchaus zu den beliebten Rollen. Auch den mitspielenden Frauen bleibt Zeit, ihr Haar wachsen zu lassen. An den Frisuren wird man künftig erkennen, wer dabei ist bei der Passion, dieser weltberühmten Aufführung der letzten Tage Jesu, die alle zehn Jahre ein oberbayerisches Dorf zu einer gigantischen Theaterfamilie verschmelzen lässt. Der „Barterlass" fällt diesmal auf den 6. März 2019. An diesem Tag beginnt die eine Geschichte.

Die andere Geschichte aber beginnt viel früher, beinahe 400 Jahre früher, im Jahr 1633. Als die Pest in Europa wütete, wandten sich die Oberammergauer in ihrer Verzweiflung an den lieben Gott und versprachen ihm ein Passionsspiel, wenn er sie nur von der Seuche erlöse. Der Legende nach starb nach dem Gelübde kein einziger Bewohner mehr am Schwarzen Tod. So spielen sie seit 1634 die Passion im entschleunigten Rhythmus von zehn Jahren. Mitmachen darf nur, wer im Ort geboren ist oder seit mehr als zwanzig Jahren dort lebt. Die Jesus-Darsteller sind also Oberammergauer, der Bühnenbildner, die Schneiderinnen, der Chor, das Orchester, die Kartenabreißer auch. Sie sind Studierende, Beamte, Architekten, Forstingenieure, Bildhauer, eine ist Flugbegleiterin, der Pontius Pilatus führt ein Hotel im Ort. Was sie nicht sind: professionelle Schauspieler. Natürlich ist es verrückt, dass ausgerechnet Laien die hochtrabendsten Texte sprechen, aber normal ist an der Passion sowieso wenig.

Ihr Spielleiter Christian Stückl ist so oberammergauerisch, wie es nur geht. Er ist 1961 geboren, in einem Gasthof aufgewachsen, wo er als Kind schon den Großen lauschte, wie sie über die Passion diskutierten, und wo er in der Gaststube Theaterstücke einstudierte, wenn seine Eltern im November in den Urlaub fuhren. Stückl, der gelernte Schnitzer, ist im Hauptberuf Regisseur und Intendant des Münchner Volkstheaters. Als Spielleiter der Passionsspiele muss er jeden, der mitmachen will, auch unterbringen, so will es das sogenannte „Spielrecht". Von den rund 5400 Einwohnern sind diesmal knapp 2100 bei der Passion dabei, die meisten auf und viele hinter der Bühne. Wer weggezogen war, kehrt für die Passion nach Oberammergau zurück. Wer dort wohnt, baut sein Leben um die Passion herum. Unvorstellbar, das Ereignis zu verpassen.

Das Haarewachsenlassen ist dabei mehr als das Kultivieren biblischer Frisuren. Jeder Zentimeter markiert ein Stück gemeinsam zurückgelegten Weges. Zehn Jahre fast haben sie darauf gewartet. Die letzte Passion

Da stehen sie nun, die frisch Auserkorenen, und vor ihnen Spielleiter Christian Stückl.

Here they are, the newly chosen ones, and director Christian Stückl in front of them.

parts is played by two actors. The director decides, who gets which part, drawing the lot decides, who plays the premiere; after that, the actors take turns.

Cengiz Görürs' parents are from Turkey; his father owns the hotel "Ammergauer Hof" right next to the train station. "It's the first time ever that a Muslim plays a main part in the Passion Play. It's insane that Christian thinks I can do this!" he says. A Muslim plays the man who betrayed Jesus. Some external observers consider this very modern; others think it's rather mean. It will go through the media, but this cast decision is typical for Christian Stückl, who likes to do things from time to time that Oberammergau might call revolutionary.

Looking at it from the city of Munich, Oberammergau is far away and way off, far behind the end of the Autobahn. You reach the town via a steep serpentine road. Behind its last turn, you see the Kofel, its local mountain with a summit that resembles a defiantly stretched-up nose. It looks stubborn, just like some of the locals. Besides the Passion Play, Oberammergau is also famous for its "Lüftlmalerei", the typical fresco paintings, its large open-air public pool and its woodcarving school. And there are plenty of splendid souvenir shops that spread a cozy, almost Christmas-like atmosphere all year long with their nativity scenes and holy figures in the shop windows. Busses full of Asian tourists usually stop here on their way from or to Linderhof Castle, others come to go hiking in the Ammergau Alps or skiing in winter. The town lives off the people who come to visit it. And off the Passion Play.

For the 42nd Passion Play from May to October 2020, half a million visitors are expected to come to town, half of them from abroad. Travel groups from the US and Australia have booked tickets for the play. During 109 performances the viewers want to sit on the around 4,500 seats in the Passion Play Theatre and watch someone, who pretends to be Jesus, hangs on the cross, dies and rises from the dead.

2010 ist lang her. Zur Erinnerung: Damals war Thomas Müller bester Nachwuchsspieler bei der Fußball-WM und Lena Meyer-Landrut gewann den Eurovision Song Contest. Und Cengiz Görür war zehn Jahre alt.

Am Tag des Haar- und Barterlasses trägt er noch Undercut, bei jeder Gelegenheit wuschelt er sich durchs Haupthaar. Er spielt den Judas. Davon hat er wie alle anderen schon im Oktober 2018 erfahren, bei der Spielerverkündung, als man vor großem Publikum und neugieriger Presse seinen Namen in Schönschrift mit Kreide an eine große Tafel vor dem Passionstheater malte. Alle 21 Hauptrollen der Passion sind doppelt besetzt. Wer welche Rolle spielt, entscheidet der Spielleiter, wer die Premiere spielt, entscheidet das Los, danach wechseln sich die Darsteller ab.

Cengiz Görürs Eltern kommen aus der Türkei, seinem Vater gehört das Hotel „Ammergauer Hof" gleich neben dem Bahnhof. „Es ist die erste Hauptrolle, die je ein Muslim in der Passion spielt. Wahnsinn, dass Christian mir das zutraut!", sagt er. Ein Muslim als Jesus-Verräter. Manche auswärtigen Beobachter finden das sehr modern, andere ein wenig fies. Es wird durch die Presse gehen, aber diese Besetzung passt zu Christian Stückl, der ganz gern mal Dinge tut, die man in Oberammergau als revolutionär bezeichnen könnte.

Von München aus betrachtet liegt Oberammergau dort, wo die Autobahn längst zu Ende ist. Ins Dorf fährt man über eine steile Serpentinenstraße, hinter deren letzter Windung man schließlich den Kofel sieht, den Hausberg. Ein Gipfel wie eine sich trotzig reckende Nase. Stur, wie der ein oder andere Dorfbewohner. Der Ort ist neben der Passion auch für seine Lüftlmalereien bekannt, für ein sehr großes Freibad und für seine Schnitzschule. Groß ist die Dichte an prallvollen Souvenirshops, die das ganze Jahr lang eine fast weihnachtliche Atmosphäre verströmen mit ihren Krippenszenen und Heiligenfiguren im Schaufenster. Busse mit asiatischen Touristen stoppen hier normalerweise auf ihrem Weg von oder nach Schloss Linderhof, andere kommen zum Wandern in den Ammergauer Alpen, im Winter zum Skifahren. Das Dorf lebt von den Leuten, die kommen. Und von der Passion.

Für die 42. Passionsspiele von Mai bis Oktober 2020 werden eine halbe Million Besucher erwartet, die Hälfte aus dem Ausland, Reisegruppen aus den USA und Australien sind angemeldet. Bei 109 Vorstellungen wollen die Zuschauer auf den rund 4500 Plätzen im Passionstheater sitzen und einen, der so tut, als sei er Jesus, am Kreuz hängen, sterben und wiederauferstehen sehen.

Jede große Rolle ist doppelt besetzt, die Spieler wechseln sich bei den Vorstellungen ab.

Each main role is double staffed; the actors take turns for the performances.

Rund 1500 Kostüme wurden allein für diese Passion neu geschneidert; in der sogenannten „Flügelei" entstehen Engelsflügel.

About 1,500 costumes have been made for this Passion Play alone; in the so-called "Flügelei" angel wings are created.

Scene 2
The Preparations

September 2019, in the garden of Gethsemane in Jerusalem. It's day five of a trip through Israel that Christian Stückl takes with his crew. Back then, not even the Chinese knew of the existence of Covid-19. All actors in main roles are part of the travel group along with the major, a theologian and Stückl himself, of course. Even in the greatest heat he wears the same clothes day in and day out: a blue shirt, jeans, and his "Haferl" shoes, no sunglasses, cigarette. The director rushes his crew through excavations, desert valleys, and churches. A visit to Yad Vashem, a talk with the Holocaust survivor Abba Naor. They engage in discussion, wherever they are – or rather, it's Stückl who is constantly discussing. About what Jesus would have done, what miracles actually are, what was radical about Jesus.

Cengiz Görür looks just as tired as the disciples must have looked a long time ago when they were supposed to keep watch with Jesus. "To be honest, I don't really know the story," he says, standing in the shade of an olive tree. For Stückl it's not important if his actors are well versed in the Bible, it's their talent that counts. And the next months will show that Görür is a very talented actor.

In the Passion Play Theatre, which used to be a sacrosanct place only to be entered every ten years, Stückl organizes summer theatre today to bring the place to life between the Passion Plays. There the people from Oberammergau play Shakespeare and Schiller, they sing opera and invite various bands for concerts. One year before the Passion Play, the traditional "Plague Play" is put on stage, which tells the story of the vow taken in

Szene 2:
Die Vorbereitungen

September 2019, Garten Gethsemane in Jerusalem. Es ist der fünfte Tag einer Reise durch Israel, die Spielleiter Stückl mit seiner Truppe unternimmt. Von Covid-19 haben da noch nicht einmal die Chinesen gehört. Die Hauptrollen sind in Israel dabei, der Bürgermeister, Theologen und allen voran Stückl, der auch bei größter Hitze immer das Gleiche trägt: blaues Hemd zu Jeans und Haferlschuhen, keine Sonnenbrille, Zigarette. Der Spielleiter treibt seine Leute durch Ausgrabungsstätten, Wüstentäler, Kirchen. Besuch von Yad Vashem, Gespräch mit dem Holocaust-Überlebenden Abba Naor. Überall diskutieren sie, besser gesagt, diskutiert Stückl. Darüber, wie Jesus gewirkt haben muss. Was Wunder eigentlich sein sollen. Was an ihm radikal war. „Nachher ratsch mer noch ein bisserl", sagt er zuverlässig am Ende des täglichen Zwölf-Stunden-Programms.

Cengiz Görür sieht so müde aus, wie damals die Jünger ausgesehen haben müssen, die mit Jesus im Garten Gethsemane wachen sollten: „Ehrlich gesagt kenne ich diese Geschichten kaum", sagt er im Schatten eines Olivenbäumchens. Stückl geht es bei seinen Spielern nicht um Bibelfestigkeit, sondern um Talent. Und dass Görür ein sehr großes Spielertalent hat, das werden die kommenden Monate zeigen.

Im Passionstheater, früher ein sakrosankter Ort, der nur alle zehn Jahre betreten werden durfte, macht Stückl auch zwischen den Passionen Sommertheater, damit Leben ins Haus kommt. Das Dorf spielt dann Shakespeare, Schiller, singt Opern, lädt Bands ein. Solch ein riesiges Theater einfach jahrelang leer herumstehen zu lassen wäre doch Blödsinn. Ein Jahr vor der Passion findet traditionell das „Pestspiel" statt, das die Geschichte des Gelübdes von 1633 erzählt. Spätestens dann beginnt das Gemunkel: Der spielt doch gut, wäre der nicht was für den Jesus? Wirklich passionsfrei hat Oberammergau eigentlich nie. Stückl sowieso nicht.

November 2019. In der sogenannten „Flügelei" verbringen Künstlerinnen ihre Tage damit, Tausende Federn zu bügeln und zu riesigen Engelsflügeln zusammenzukleben. In der Schneiderei rattern seit Wochen Nähmaschinen. Rund 1500 Kostüme müssen neu geschneidert werden, bis auf etwas Römerzubehör und ein paar Sandalen wird nichts von 2010 verwendet, das

STÜCKLS PLAN UND GOTTES BEITRAG

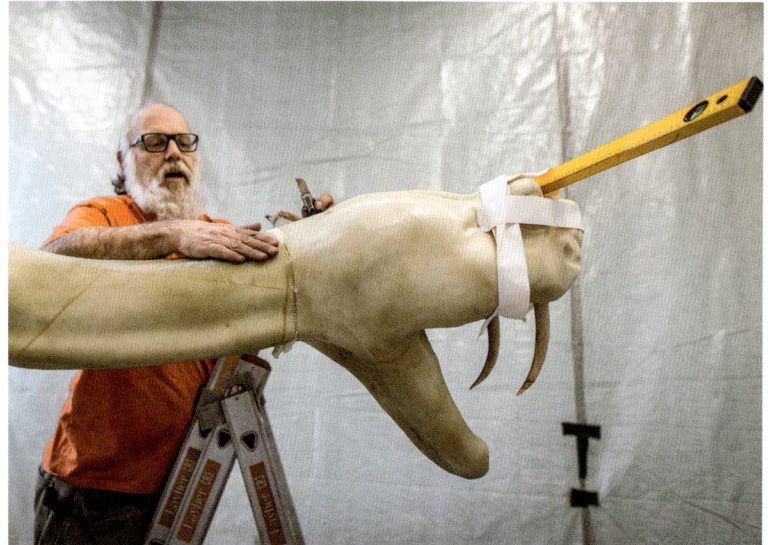

1633. By then, at the latest, rumors have started: He is a good actor, wouldn't he be a good Jesus? Oberammergau is actually always involved with the Passion Play somehow. And so is Stückl.

November 2019. In the so called "Flügelei" (wing factory) numerous artists spend their days ironing thousands of feathers and sticking them together to create huge angel wings. In the tailor shops the sewing machines have been humming for months. About 1,500 new costumes must be made, hardly anything from 2010 is used. Stage and costume designer Stefan Hageneier has created a whole new concept. A few of the old costumes might be reworked for art projects or kept privately; some actors still have their costume at home and wear it as a dressing gown now. For one of the passion plays, Stefan Hageneier bought heaps of sandals in Jerusalem; this time, he organized some old carpets in Anatolia; in India, he ordered block print fabrics. This year the costumes are mostly kept in muted colors: brown, black, sandy, khaki; nothing flashy – Jesus' followers are supposed to look like ordinary, outdoor people from the countryside. Just like those that Jesus inspired back then.

A parallel project is the creation of the "living pictures", the "Tableaux Vivantes" that the Passion Play is also famous for. They frame the twelve play scenes and show scenes from the Old Testament. Real people reenact these scenes and stand motionless for a few minutes while the choir sings. Stefan Hageneier wants to set the focus on the flight of the people of Israel. There are scenes from the five books of Moses, the burning bush, the tablets of the Ten Commandments, and the dance around a huge golden calf. After it was finished, however, the calf had to be hollowed out and cut a bit, because at first, it was too big and heavy to be moved on stage.

Up until a major reconstruction in 2019, there was the house of Pontius Pilate on one side of the stage and the house of the priest Annas on the other. Stückl and Hageneier thought this was not flexible enough. Some locals vehemently opposed the reconstruction – after all, where was Pontius Pilate to come out from, when there was no house anymore? The Passion Play has always been a rather naturalistic presentation. That is, if you want to call a story without much historic evidence naturalistic that revolves around a Jew, who is crucified and then rises from the dead. Stückl's team won and now the stage is meant to resemble a large temple complex in Jerusalem, an open place, where people come together. And also, the place that, according to the Bible, Jesus visits at some point.

Konzept von Bühnen- und Kostümbildner Stefan Hageneier ist ganz neu. Alte Kostüme werden höchstens für Kunstprojekte weiterverwendet, oder privat: Manche Darsteller haben sie behalten und tragen sie jetzt zu Hause als Morgenmäntel. Einmal hat Stefan Hageneier haufenweise Sandalen in Jerusalem gekauft, diesmal organisierte er alte Teppiche in Anatolien, in Indien ließ er Stoffe mit Blockprint herstellen. Die Farben der Darsteller-Kostüme sind diesmal gedeckt: braun, schwarz, sandfarben, erdig. Nichts, was rausknallt, die Gefolgschaft von Jesus soll nach einfachen Menschen von draußen aussehen, vom Land. Eben wie jene, die Jesus begeistert hat.

Parallel entstehen die „Lebenden Bilder" neu, die „Tableaux Vivantes", für die die Passion auch berühmt ist und die die zwölf Spielszenen umrahmen. Sie zeigen Szenen aus dem Alten Testament, von echten Menschen nachgestellt, die ein paar Minuten regungslos verharren, während der Chor die Szene besingt. Stefan Hageneier will den Schwerpunkt auf das Thema Flucht des Volks Israel lenken. Man sieht Szenen aus den fünf Büchern Mose, den brennenden Dornbusch, die Tafeln mit den zehn Geboten, den Tanz um ein riesiges Goldenes Kalb. Wobei das Kalb nach seiner Fertigstellung noch ausgehöhlt und etwas abgeschnitten werden musste, weil es so schwer auf der Bühne zu bewegen war.

Bis zu einem größeren Umbau 2019 war auf der einen Seite der Bühne das Haus von Pontius Pilatus, das von Priester Annas auf der anderen. Stückl und Hageneier war das zu festgelegt. Manch Oberammergauer sträubte sich gegen den Umbau, denn wo solle der Pilatus rauskommen, wenn er kein Haus mehr habe? Die Passion ist seit jeher ein recht naturalistisches Spiel, sofern man bei einer historisch kaum belegten Geschichte um einen Juden, dessen Kreuzigung und anschließender Auferstehung überhaupt von Naturalismus sprechen kann. Das Team um Stückl setzte sich durch, jetzt soll die Bühne eher an eine große Tempelanlage in Jerusalem erinnern, ein offener Ort, an dem die Menschen zusammenkommen können. Und der Ort, an den Jesus laut Bibel eines Tages kommt.

Für die Lebenden Bilder bauen die Künstler ein Goldenes Kalb, die Paradiesschlange und natürlich den Baum der Erkenntnis.

For the living pictures the artists have built a golden calf, the serpent from paradise and the tree of knowledge, of course.

Scene 3:
Criticism – the Passion Play and Antisemitism

The first snow starts falling in November in Oberammergau, a normal situation in an Alpine village, where everyone wears warm boots and ski jackets all winter long anyway. Stückl, however, wears the same clothes as usual: a jeans, shirt, Haferl shoes, and a cigarette. It seems that the only times he wears a jacket are, when he happens to come across one on his hurried walks through the theatre.

The theatre was built in 1830 on the so-called Passion Field on the edge of town because back then, the priest was fed up with everyone trampling around his cemetery during the passion plays as it was common practice at the time. Over the years, the theatre was remodeled several times and got its present form in 1930 as the largest open-air stage in the world with a roofed auditorium. On the back wall of the theatre, Stückl has his office, which he calls his "atelier" with a large glass front. Many, many nights people can see him sitting there bent over some texts, smoking. Anybody can look in and come in, too. That is important in a place like Oberammergau, where the Passion Play belongs to and concerns everybody. If Germany has 80 million national soccer coaches that always know better, Oberammergau has 5,400 play directors.

It's the last day of a short time-out that Christian Stückl has retreated to. Two rabbis and a religious scholar have flown in from the US, and now they are all sitting together around the large wooden table in Stückl's atelier to work through his current text version of the text line by line. The small room is filled with smoke, Stückl needs about one cigarette per thought. One of the rabbis notes that in 2010, the people of Jerusalem were all dressed in the same dark color during the scene when Jesus was sentenced to death. That seems like a general suspicion, he says, and shows the crowd as a mob. Stückl thinks about this objection and then agrees with it. The visitors also criticize the living pictures of 2010. Back then, stage designer Stefan Hageneier wanted to tell the story from a post-Easter point of view as he explains. There is a dove, a cross and many other symbols of Christianity. In the eyes of the visitors, these symbols distract the audience from the fact that Jesus was a Jew, and according to what is known today, was not planning at all to found a new religion.

Szene 3:
Die Kritik – die Passion und der Antisemitismus

Der erste Schnee fällt im November in Oberammergau, nicht der Rede wert in einem Alpendorf, in dem im Winter sowieso alle durchgehend in dicken Stiefeln und Skijacken herumlaufen. Nur Stückl trägt wie immer Jeans, Hemd, Haferlschuhe, Zigarette. Eine Jacke scheint er nur anzuziehen, wenn er beim Herumeilen im Theater zufällig eine zu greifen kriegt.

1830 wurde auf der sogenannten Passionswiese am Ortsrand das Theater errichtet, weil der Pfarrer es satthatte, dass man für die Spiele immer auf seinem Friedhof herumtrampelte, wie es bis dahin üblich war. Nach mehreren Umbauten hat das Theater seit 1930 seine heutige Form und ist die größte Freiluftbühne mit überdachtem Zuschauerraum weltweit. An der Rückseite des Theaters hat Stückl sein Büro, das „Atelier", mit großer Glasfront. Sehr viele Abende sieht man ihn dort sitzen, gebeugt über einen Text, rauchend. Jeder kann reinschauen und theoretisch auch reinkommen. Das ist wichtig an einem Ort, wo die Passion Allgemeingut ist. Wenn Deutschland 80 Millionen Bundestrainer hat, die alles besser wissen, hat Oberammergau 5400 Spielleiter.

Es ist der letzte Tag einer kleinen Klausur, in die sich Christian Stückl begeben hat. Aus den USA sind zwei Rabbiner und ein Religionswissenschaftler angereist und gehen am großen Holztisch des Ateliers mit Stückl Zeile um Zeile seiner aktuellen Textfassung durch. Im Büro steht der Rauch, pro Gedanke braucht Stückl etwa eine Zigarette. Einer der Rabbis stellt fest, dass im Volk Jerusalems 2010 bei der Verurteilung Jesu alle in derselben dunklen Farbe gekleidet waren. Das wirke pauschal verdächtigend, die Menge als Mob. Stückl prüft diesen Einwand, gibt ihm schließlich recht. Sie kritisieren auch die Lebenden Bilder von 2010. Bühnenbildner Stefan Hageneier wollte, erklärt er, alles aus einer nachösterlichen Sicht erzählen. So tauchte eine Taube auf, ein Kreuz, viele Symbole, christliche Symbole. Die ablenkten, finden die Gäste, von der Tatsache, dass Jesus Jude war und nach allem, was man weiß, überhaupt nicht vorhatte, eine Religion zu gründen.

Der Passionstext ist ein Sammelsurium aus alten Passionsspielen aus der Region, Dichtungen von Mönchen, etwa aus dem benachbarten Kloster Ettal, aus Texten des Neuen Testaments, ein „Bibel-Potpourri", nennt es Stückl. Der Text wurde über die Jahrhunderte immer ein wenig angepasst, doch seit Stückl Spielleiter ist, ändert er ihn jede Passion.

Eines seiner wichtigsten Anliegen dabei: den Text von jeglichem Antijudaismus befreien. Der steckte in etlichen Passagen und hat viele Passionsjahrzehnte lang niemanden gestört. Der sogenannte „Blutruf" etwa aus dem Matthäusevangelium. Kurz nachdem Pontius Pilatus seine viel zitierten Hände in Unschuld gewaschen hat, sagt er: „Ich bin unschuldig am Blut dieses Menschen, das ist eure Sache." Dann geht es weiter: „Da rief das ganze Volk: Sein Blut über uns und unsere Kinder!" Auch aus Bibelstellen wie dieser leitet sich ein bis heute währender, verheerender christlicher Antisemitismus ab. Die Stelle wird als Beleg für die Schuld der Juden am Tod von Jesus benutzt, als angebliche Übernahme der Verantwortung. Früher kam es regelmäßig

The current text of the Passion Play is a hodgepodge of texts from old passion plays from the region, poems written by monks, e.g., from the neighboring Ettal monastery, and texts from the New Testament, a "Bible potpourri", as Stückl calls it. Over the centuries, the text has only been adjusted slightly for every play, but since Stückl has taken over the job as director, he changes it for every new play.

In that, one of his main concerns is to clear out the text from any form of Anti-Judaism. This could be found in many passages of the text, a fact that didn't really bother anyone for many, many decades. One example is the so-called "blood curse" from the Gospel of Matthew. Shortly after Pontius Pilate has washed his frequently quoted hands in innocence, he says: "I am innocent of this man's blood; see to it yourselves." Then, it goes on: "All the people answered: His blood be on us and on our children!" It is also from Bible verses like this one, that a disastrous Christian Antisemitism can be derived. This verse is used as evidence that the Jews are guilty of Jesus' death, and that they allegedly take responsibility for it. In earlier years, pogroms and assaults on Jews occurred regularly everywhere in the country after the Passion Play. The above quote in the Bible was also part of the Oberammergau Passion Play, of course – and no one questioned it.

Stückl sees all these devastating failures. He seeks the dialogue with Jewish people and wants to increase his own and everyone's awareness of everything that is presented on stage – with costumes and texts. As early as 1990, he plans to ban the blood curse from the text, but his theological consultant doesn't allow it. Back then, this consultant is assigned by the Catholic church to assist and advise the young Stückl to make sure that his reforms are not too bold for the church. "Therefore, I gave this sentence to the three oldest men on stage, they all had false teeth and mumbled the words so that nobody in the audience really heard them." In the Passion Play of 2000, the sentence was gone.

Stückl shows Jesus as the Jew that he was. Jesus prays in Hebrew; the disciples call him "Rabbi" and wear kippahs. For the play 2010, the musical director Markus Zwink composed a Hebrew song, the "Sch'ma Israel"; it sets one of the most important Jewish prayers to music. The Jews are not a closed group anymore, they also engage in heated discussions and cannot agree if Jesus should be crucified or not. And Judas is shown as a disappointed disciple, not as a cold traitor.

Stückl's efforts are seen and respected. In 2020, he receives the Abraham Geiger Award, and in 2021 the Buber-Rosenzweig Medal for his honest attempts to maintain a dialogue between Christians and Jews and his continuous work on the text, scenes, costumes, and stage. And still, he knows that he must keep up his work against Antisemitism in the Passion Play. Whenever you tell the story of the passion of Christ, he says, you risk reproducing Antisemitism.

nach Passionsspielen überall im Land zu Pogromen und Angriffen auf Juden. Selbstverständlich kam der Satz auch in der Oberammergauer Passion vor, unhinterfragt.

Als Hitler 1934 die Spiele zum 300-jährigen Bestehen besucht, ist das Dorf entzückt, die Passion wird „reichswichtig". Nach dem Krieg will zwar niemand mehr was mit der Nazi-Zeit zu tun haben, mit einer Aufarbeitung aber noch weniger. Noch 1950 und 1960 wird ein Nazi-Sympathisant zum Jesus ernannt. 1969 rufen die Anti-Defamation League und das Jewish Committee aus den USA zum Boykott der Spiele auf. Johann Georg Lang, bis 1960 Spielleiter, sagte damals zu den Antisemitismus-Vorwürfen: „Wir spielen nicht fanatisch, sondern bayerisch." Ausgerechnet der Vatikan muss progressiv einschreiten und Ende der 60er-Jahre Oberammergau auffordern, die Darstellung der Juden zu überarbeiten. 1970 entzieht der damalige Kardinal Julius Döpfner Oberammergau gar die „Missio Canonica", den Missionierungsauftrag, erst dann wird man nachdenklich.

Stückl sieht die verheerenden Versäumnisse. Er sucht das Gespräch mit Jüdinnen und Juden und will sich und andere sensibilisieren für das, was auf der Bühne, in Kostüm und Text zu sehen und hören ist. 1990 schon will er den Blutruf aus dem Text tilgen, das aber erlaubt der theologische Berater nicht, der dem jungen Stückl damals von der katholischen Kirche an die Seite gestellt wurde, um sicherzugehen, dass es nicht gar zu reformistisch zugeht. „Also hab ich den Satz den drei ältesten Männern mit Gebiss gegeben", sagt Stückl, „die haben ihn weggenuschelt, sodass ihn kaum einer hörte." Bei der Passion 2000 war der Satz dann weg.

Jesus zeigt er als den Juden, der er war. Jesus betet auf Hebräisch, die Jünger nennen ihn „Rabbi" und tragen Kippa. Für 2010 hat der musikalische Leiter Markus Zwink auch ein hebräisches Lied komponiert, das „Schma Israel", es ist die Vertonung eines wichtigen jüdischen Gebets. Die Juden sind keine geschlossene Gruppe mehr, sie diskutieren ebenfalls hitzig und sind keineswegs einig, ob Jesus hingerichtet werden soll oder nicht. Und Judas soll ein enttäuschter Jünger sein, kein kalter Verräter.

Stückls Anliegen wird ernst- und wahrgenommen. Er erhält 2020 den Abraham Geiger Preis, 2021 die Buber-Rosenzweig-Medaille für sein aufrichtiges Bemühen um einen Austausch zwischen Christen und Juden und die anhaltende Überarbeitung von Text, Szenen, Kostüm und Bühne. Trotzdem weiß er, dass sein Einsatz gegen Antisemitismus im Passionsspiel weitergehen muss. So lange man die biblische Passionsgeschichte erzähle, laufe man Gefahr, Antisemitismus zu reproduzieren.

Erste Leseprobe im Dezember 2019 (links). Stückl tauscht sich oft mit Rabbinern aus und arbeitet die antisemitische Geschichte der Spiele auf (S. 71 und rechts).

First reading rehearsal in December 2019 (left). Stückl talks to rabbis frequently and confronts the antisemitic history of the play (p. 71 and right).

Scene 4:
A Life in Oberammergau

"Hosanna!", Cengiz Görur cheers during the entry into Jerusalem; this is the first spoken word of the Passion Play after a great opening scene with the choir and a living picture. It's January 25th, 2020 and the first so-called "people rehersal" in the theatre. It smells of wet sawdust and fan heaters. In the half-open theatre, it always feels five degrees colder than outside; even for the premiere in May most people on stage will wear thermal underwear. Görur has pulled the hood of his sweater over his head. There are about 400 people in the theatre, parents are carrying their babies in slings, and children are jumping around. Mass motivator Christian Stückl speaks into the microphone: "No running in the theatre! You may only run towards Jesus." Stückl's father, Peter, is there, too. He quietly watches the crazy hustle and bustle from the edge of the stage. He is 78 years old at the time and this would be his 10th Passion Play.

In Oberammergau, life isn't measured in years but in Passion Play units. Friendships and love relationships develop during the play; it connects the very old and the very young. It gives the participants the feeling of being part of something greater than themselves. During the Passion Play, they remember why it makes sense to live in this town. Most of them don't have an answer when asked what could stop them from being part of the play. They simply cannot think of anything. Except for events of force majeure maybe such as death or illness. But that hardly ever happens, right?

Only twice, the Passion Play was canceled completely: in 1770 due to the turmoil of the Enlightenment and in 1940 during World War II. A few times, it had to be postponed, like in 1920, exactly 100 years ago, when too many men had been killed in World War I. Back then, the play was postponed to 1922. Remarkably often, however, the Passion Play was held according to schedule. Could the Passion Play be canceled this year? Unthinkable.

Im Passionstheater ist es im Winter eiskalt, Proben sind da nur in dicker Kleidung auszuhalten.

The theatre is freezing cold in winter, everybody wears warm clothes for rehearsals.

Szene 4:
Ein Oberammergauer Leben

"Hosianna!", jubelt Cengiz Görür beim Einzug nach Jerusalem, das ist das erste Wort, das in der Passion gesprochen wird, nach einer großen Eröffnungsszene mit Chor und Lebendem Bild. Es ist der 25. Januar 2020, die erste sogenannte Volksprobe im Passionstheater. Es riecht nach nassen Sägespänen und Heizlüftern. Im halb offenen Theater ist es immer gefühlte fünf Grad kälter als draußen, auch bei der Premiere im Mai wird zu Thermo-Unterwäsche geraten. Görür hat die Kapuze seines Pullis über den Kopf gezogen. 400 Menschen sind da, Eltern haben ihre Säuglinge umgeschnallt, Kinder springen herum. Massenmotivator Stückl spricht ins Mikrofon: „Rennverbot im Theater! Nur auf den Jesus zurennen dürft ihr." Auch Stückls Vater Peter ist da und betrachtet das verrückte Treiben in aller Gelassenheit von der Seite. Er ist zu der Zeit 78 Jahre alt, dies wäre seine 10. Passion.

Ein Oberammergauer Leben bemisst sich nicht in Jahren, sondern in Passionseinheiten. Die Passion stiftet Freundschaften, Liebesbeziehungen, sie verbindet die ganz Alten mit den ganz Jungen. Sie löst in den Leuten das Gefühl aus, Teil von etwas zu sein, das größer ist als sie selbst. Die Passion erinnert sie daran, warum es Sinn hat, in diesem Dorf zu leben. Die meisten stutzen, wenn man sie fragt, was sie vom Mitmachen abhalten könnte. Ihnen fällt nichts ein. Gut, abgesehen von Dingen der höheren Gewalt. Todesfälle, Krankheiten. Aber wann gibt's das schon.

Ganz ausgefallen ist die Passion nur zweimal. 1770 in den Wirren der Aufklärung und 1940, während des Zweiten Weltkriegs. Ein paar Mal kommt es zu Verschiebungen, 1920 etwa, vor genau hundert Jahren, als nach dem Ersten Weltkrieg zu viele gefallen waren, da verschob man auf 1922. Bemerkenswert oft klappt alles wie geplant. Dass die Passion diesmal ausfallen könnte? Unvorstellbar.

Scene 5:
"Heil dir, heil dir!"
The Music

Mastermind der Musik: Markus Zwink (oben) und Tenor Moritz Kugler (unten).

Mastermind of music: Markus Zwink (above) and tenor Moritz Kugler (below).

Oberammergau is probably the only town in Bavaria that has its own hymn: the "Heil dir", sung by the Passion Choir and the children on stage during the entry into Jerusalem. Every single person from Oberammergau knows it, the children learn it in kindergarten.

"Hail oh Son of David, the throne of the father is yours", it says there. This piece of music opens the Passion Play, and after it, the scenes begin. Rochus Dedler composed it in 1815 during the era of early Romanticism. Until today, Dedlers music forms the framework of the opulent Passion Play music for orchestra and choir, which is closely linked to the events on stage. Choir and orchestra accompany the "living pictures"; they comment on the scenes shown there, e.g., the expulsion from paradise, and then they prepare the next play scene.

Today, Markus Zwink is just as important as Rochus Dedler. Zwink has been the musical director of the Passion Play since 1990, and he is a pragmatic man. This year for the very first time, the prologue was canceled, a narrator who appeared between the scenes and connected the story to the living pictures. And often he gave a moral comment on what was shown there. Christian Stückl thought that the prologue was too moralistic and removed it from the text. This, however, left gaps between the scenes that had to be filled with music. So, Zwink simply composed transition pieces that gave enough time for the necessary modifications on stage.

He also wrote the "Sch'ma Israel", which sets a Hebrew prayer to music and has a slightly oriental feel to it. This fits with Stückl's attempts to focus on the fact that Jesus led the life of a Jew. For 2022 Zwink also set the stations of the cross to music and here, too, the choir sings in Hebrew: "Eli, Eli, lama sabachtani? My God, my God, why have you forsaken me?" inspired by Jesus' last words and psalm 22, that John the Evangelist used to tell the story of the crucifixion.

There are 64 choir singers, four of them soloists, as well as 60 musicians. The town supports the musical training of the soloists, but here, other than in the play, also singers and musicians who are not from Oberammergau can participate, if this means an "increase in quality". "The best trick is", says Markus Zwink, "to learn an exotic instrument. That's your ticket to the orchestra." Bassoon or oboe, for example, there are always too few of those. And so, every now and then one or two musicians from Unterammergau, too, have been able to be part of the Passion Play.

Szene 5:
„Heil dir, heil dir!" Die Musik

Oberammergau hat wohl als einziges Dorf Bayerns eine eigene Hymne. Das „Heil dir", das beim Einzug nach Jerusalem der Passionschor und die Kinder auf der Bühne singen. Jeder, wirklich jeder in Oberammergau kennt es, die Kinder lernen es schon im Kindergarten: „Heil dir, oh Davids Sohn, der Väter Thron gebühret dir", heißt es da. Das Stück eröffnet die Passion gewissermaßen, danach beginnt das Spiel. Es sind Zeilen einer Komposition von Rochus Dedler aus dem Jahr 1815, Zeit der Frühromantik. Dedlers Melodien sind bis heute das feste Gerüst der opulenten Passionsmusik für Orchester und Chor, die eng mit dem Bühnengeschehen verwoben ist. Chor und Orchester begleiten die „Lebenden Bilder", sie kommentieren die darin gezeigten Szenen – die Vertreibung aus dem Paradies etwa – und leiten dann über die nächste Spielszene.

So wichtig wie Komponist Rochus Dedler ist Markus Zwink, seit 1990 Herr der Passionsmusik – und Pragmatiker. Diesmal fällt erstmalig der Prolog weg, eine Erzählerfigur, die zwischen den Szenen auftrat und die Geschichte mit den Lebenden Bildern verband und gern mal andeutete, was man davon zu halten habe. Christian Stückl fand den Prolog zu moralisch und strich ihn aus dem Text. Nur: Jetzt waren Löcher da, die musikalisch gefüllt werden mussten. Also komponierte Zwink eben Übergänge, die die nötige Zeit für Umbauten schaffen.

Von ihm stammt auch das „Schma Israel", die orientalisch anmutende Vertonung eines hebräischen Gebets. Das passt zu Stückls Bestrebungen, das jüdische Leben zu betonen, das Jesus geführt hat. Für 2022 hat Zwink auch den Kreuzweg vertont, auch hier singt der Chor wieder hebräisch: „Eli, Eli, lama sabachtani? Mein Gott, mein Gott, warum hast du mich verlassen?", angelehnt an Jesus' letzte Worte beziehungsweise an den Psalm 22, den der Evangelist Johannes benutzt hat, um die Kreuzigungsgeschichte zu erzählen.

64 Chorsänger sind dabei, davon vier Solisten, und 60 Musiker. Die Gemeinde unterstützt die musikalische Ausbildung der Solisten, trotzdem dürfen hier im Gegensatz zum Spiel auch Nicht-Oberammergauer mitmachen, wenn es der „Qualitätssteigerung" dient. „Der beste Trick", sagt Markus Zwink, „ist, ein exotisches Instrument zu lernen, das verschafft Zugang zum Orchester", Fagott oder Oboe zum Beispiel, an denen mangelt es chronisch. Auf diese Weise war sogar der ein oder andere Unterammergauer schon bei der Passion dabei.

Scene 6:
The Chosen Ones

Mary must represent. That's part of the Passion Play; so, one evening in mid-February 2020, Eva Reiser is sitting at a table in the Bavarian Representation Office in Berlin. A committee from Oberammergau has been invited to talk about the Passion Play in front of ministry officials and some curious Bavarians in exile. The closer the premiere gets, the more frequently they have appointments like this – the interest is enormous. The infection rates of the new virus are rising, but nobody thinks it possible that this could have any serious consequences on the world. "Eva Reiser plays Mother Mary, and when she is not on stage, she is often above the clouds as well – she works as a flight attendant," the moderator introduces her proudly. Eva laughs politely. Mary is an icon; every woman who plays her automatically becomes celestial.

Eva Reiser's father died a few months earlier, she accompanied him during his last days. "This experience has helped me a lot to understand the part of Mary better," Reiser says. She knows what it feels like when you have to let someone go. Playing this role, she says, is a bit like therapy for her. She has taken leave for the Passion Play – it's hard to work part-time when you are flying. The organization Oberammergau Kultur, which organizes the Passion Play, remunerates every actor to compensate for the lost earnings.

Ash Wednesday 2020, 10 o'clock, cross rehearsal with Jesus actor Frederik Mayet. Around him, workers are painting the set, there is a bucket full of donkey manure in the corner. Mayet, wearing jeans and a sweatshirt, uses a ladder to climb the standing cross and has himself tied up. For this to be as pain-free as possible, the cross must be well adjusted to the actor. But this year, the two Jesus actors, who are of different height, share one cross. Otherwise, there would be too much stuff lying around in the theatre, one of the carpenters comments while he is working on his own cross. He plays one of the thieves who are crucified next to Jesus. A few tricks and gimmicks are necessary for the crucifixion, of course, hooks, straps, belts and such. Still, Mayet says, whenever they erect the cross with him hanging on it, four and a half meters high, he fears for a moment that he is about to fall forward into the audience.

There used to be Jesus actors who took the godliness of their role a bit too seriously. There is the notorious Anton Lang, who played Jesus three times in a row; the last time, he was over 40 years old. He identified so strongly with this part that, even in the years between the Passion Plays, he rarely cut his hair or beard, and was happy to bless people when asked. For some people, a Jesus-actor fells more real than no savior at all. That's also why many visitors want to have their picture taken with one of the Jesus actors, some want to touch them. Frederik Mayet, born in 1980, knows all this – he was Jesus in 2010. Stückl gave him the part again, because he "hasn't gotten it into his bones yet".

Irgendwo müssen sie ja liegen, die Kreuze. Hier im Gang des Passionstheaters.

The crosses have to be stored somewhere – for now it's the hallway of the theatre.

Zweimal Gottesmutter: Andrea Hecht (links) und Eva Reiser spielen die Maria.

Two times the Blessed Mother: Andrea Hecht (left) and Eva Reiser both play Mary.

Szene 6:
Die Auserwählten

Maria muss repräsentieren. Das gehört auch zur Passion, deshalb sitzt Eva Reiser an einem Abend Mitte Februar 2020 in der Bayerischen Vertretung in Berlin. Ein Komitee aus Oberammergau ist eingeladen, vor Ministerialbeamten und neugierigen Exil-Bayern über die Spiele zu sprechen. Je näher die Premiere rückt, desto häufiger haben sie solche Termine, das Interesse ist riesig. Die Infektionszahlen mit dem zu dieser Zeit noch „neuartigen" Virus steigen zwar, aber niemand hält es für möglich, dass so was ernsthafte Konsequenzen für die Welt haben könnte. „Eva Reiser spielt die Muttergottes, und auch sonst schwebt sie über den Wolken, denn sie ist Flugbegleiterin", stellt sie der Moderator stolz vor. Sie lacht höflich. Maria ist eine Ikone, jede Frau, die sie spielt, selbst automatisch überirdisch.

Ein paar Monate zuvor starb Eva Reisers Vater, sie war bei ihm in den letzten Tagen. „Ich spüre, dass mir das die Rolle der Maria sehr nahebringt", sagt Reiser. Sie weiß, wie es ist, jemanden gehen lassen zu müssen. Die Rolle zu spielen, sagt sie, sei auch ein bisschen Therapie. Sie hat sich für die Passion beurlauben lassen, Fliegen geht schlecht in Teilzeit. Der Eigenbetrieb Oberammergau Kultur, Veranstalter der Passion, zahlt jedem Spieler ein Honorar, um den Verdienstausfall im Beruf, so gut es geht, zu kompensieren.

Aschermittwoch 2020, 10 Uhr, Kreuzprobe mit Jesus-Darsteller Frederik Mayet. Zwischen malernden Handwerkern und einem Eimer Eselkot steigt er in Jeans und Pulli über eine Leiter ans stehende Kreuz und lässt sich festmachen. Damit es sich halbwegs schmerzfrei hängt, muss ein Kreuz gut angepasst sein. Die beiden unterschiedlich großen Jesus-Darsteller aber teilen sich diesmal ein Kreuz. Sonst liege hier im Theater ja so viel herum, sagt einer der Schreiner, der gerade an seinem eigenen Kreuz bohrt, er spielt einen der Schächer, die neben Jesus hängen. Natürlich wird bei der Kreuzigung mit Tricks gearbeitet, mit Haken und Gurten. Mayet sagt, wenn er dann aufgerichtet wird, viereinhalb Meter hoch hängend, denke er trotzdem jedes Mal, er kippe gleich vornüber in den Zuschauerraum.

Es gab schon Jesus-Darsteller, die es gar zu ernst genommen haben mit der Frömmigkeit. Berühmtberüchtigt ist der Jesus-Darsteller Anton Lang, der ganze dreimal den Jesus spielte, auch noch mit über 40 Jahren. Er identifizierte sich, heißt es, so stark mit der Rolle, dass er auch in den passionsfreien Jahren Haare und Bart lang wachsen ließ und auch gern mal Menschen segnete. Ein gespielter Heiland ist für viele eben immer noch echter als gar kein Heiland. Deshalb wollen sich erfahrungsgemäß viele Besucher mit einem der beiden Darsteller fotografieren lassen, manche wollen ihn berühren. Frederik Mayet, Jahrgang 1980, kennt das Begehr schon, denn auch 2010 war er Jesus. Er durfte noch mal ran, sagt Stückl, weil er sich damals „nicht richtig freigespielt" habe.

Scene 7:
The Unthinkable

On March 12th, 2020, the actors and Christian Stückl gather on the center stage of the Passion Play Theatre. They have enough room there to keep distance, as is required these days, although just a few weeks ago, they were all still so close to each other. They are in the middle of shooting the pictures for an opulent photo book, a popular souvenir, the Panini album of the Passion Play, if you like. This new virus has spread faster than they thought, people have died, and there are infections in their own district Garmisch-Partenkirchen as well. This is simply too much irony of the fate, they think, that it could be a plague out of all things that might put an end to all their great plans. Since it was a plague in the first place that initiated their vow. Eva Reiser arrives from the airport. She is nervous, and keeps washing her hands. "I don't want to be the one bringing the plague into our town," she says. Stückl motivates his actors and tells them at the end of their meeting: "We will play!", and "Learn your lines!" They go home, unsure what the future will bring. A few days later, on March 19th, 2020, the Passion Play is canceled. Postponed. To a date that feels so incredibly far away: May 2022.

Then, there is silence.

Scene 8:
The Resurrection

In January 2022, they all meet again – the Jesus actors and Mary actresses, the Romans, the mob – for the second first reading rehearsal. They are vaccinated and tested; everybody is wearing a mask – the new normal. They are talking and laughing together, trying to get close again.

Two years have passed. In two years, one can have children, get married, get separated, finish studying, drop out of a vocational training program, elect a new German chancellor, get ill. Some of the disciples did not come back, new actors have joined the group, a few of the older actors have passed away. "We will play," Stückl says. "How we will play, nobody knows." In January 2022, large-scale events are still only allowed without audiences, but Stückl hopes that this will have changed by May. So, maybe they will play in smaller groups or in front of fewer viewers, one has become flexible, after all. Christian Stückl is a man who doesn't get out of whack easily, or so it seems. He spent the last two years talking to politicians about culture and Corona and reopening the new "Volkstheater" in Munich, which he also manages. So, nobody is seriously worried anymore in January. After

Schwer vorstellbar, dass etwas die Oberammergauer Passion erschüttern könnte. Bis zum Frühjahr 2020 (links). Große Pause: Stückl verlässt das Theater (oben).

Hard to imagine that anything could bring down the Oberammergau Passion Play. Up until spring 2020 (left). Lunch break: Stückl is leaving the theatre (above).

Szene 7:
Das Unvorstellbare

Am 12. März 2020 kommen die Spieler und Christian Stückl auf der Mittelbühne des Passionstheaters zusammen. Da ist genug Platz, Abstand zu halten, so, wie man das jetzt neuerdings machen muss, obwohl da gerade noch so viel Nähe zwischen ihnen war. Sie stecken mitten in den Aufnahmen für einen opulenten Bildband, ein beliebtes Souvenir, das Panini-Album der Passion, wenn man so will. Dieses Virus hatte sich doch schneller verbreitet, erste Menschen sind gestorben, auch im Landkreis Garmisch-Partenkirchen gibt es Infizierte. So viel Ironie des Schicksals kann es doch gar nicht geben, denken sie, dass es ausgerechnet eine Seuche sein würde, die alle schönen Pläne durchkreuzt, wo die Passion doch genau deshalb begründet wurde, als Triumph über eine Seuche. Eva Reiser kommt vom Flughafen. Sie ist nervös, wäscht sich ständig die Hände: „Ich will nicht die sein, die die Pest ins Dorf bringt", sagt sie. Stückl motiviert seine Spieler und Spielerinnen und sagt bei dem Treffen zum Abschied noch: „Wir werden spielen." Und: „Lernt euren Text!" Sie gehen auseinander, verunsichert. Ein paar Tage später, am 19. März 2020, werden die Passionsspiele abgesagt. Verschoben. Auf ein Datum, das sich ungeheuer fern anfühlt: Mai 2022.

Dann folgt eine lange Stille.

2022 läuft alles mit Abstand, dafür aber mit Kostüm. Hier: Josef von Arimathäa (Christian Bierling, Mitte) und zwei heitere Henker (unten).

In 2022 they have to keep their distance – but they can wear costumes again. Here: Joseph of Arimathea (Christian Bierling, center) and two cheerful executioners (below).

all, they have already been through the worst possible thing, they say – the cancellation.

Therefore, in March 2022, Jesus actor Frederik Mayet is sitting in the reopened canteen of the Passion Play Theatre watching the hustle and bustle in the room: Mary and Mary Magdalene toast with a glass of sparkling wine, and one of the executioners orders goulash soup. A normal day of rehearsal. Mayets dreadful appearance, however, is all but normal, and everybody who enters the room has a comment for him: He has dark rings under his eyes, straggly hair, and his forehead is bloodstained. It's his second first day in the Jesus-look. The make-up artist has been very thorough to turn him into the suffering Christ. She spread dirt and theatre blood on his body. These are the weeks in which – once again – the opulent pictures are taken for the official photo book. Beneath his scratchy red linen robe, Mayet is only wearing a white loincloth. Having it put on him is a special procedure because the loincloth also includes the hidden safety belt for the crucifixion. He and his fellow Jesus actor Rochus Rückel call this procedure "being diapered". Then Mayet is called out via loudspeaker for the next photo, and he scurries off to the stage.

Every now and then, the actors remind each other that it was during these photo shoots in 2020 that the Passion Play was canceled. When the symbolic date, March 19th, is behind them, everybody seems relieved. It feels as if now, finally, the next chapter can be opened They haven't kept one single photo from 2020.

Szene 8:
Die Wiederauferstehung

Anfang Januar 2022 haben sie sich wieder getroffen, die Jesusse und Marias, die Römer, die Rottler, zur zweiten ersten Leseprobe. Geimpft, getestet, mit Maske. Dinge, die längst niemand mehr erwähnenswert findet. Sie haben gelacht, sich angenähert, etwas gefremdelt. Zwei Jahre sind vergangen. In zwei Jahren kann man Kinder kriegen, heiraten, sich trennen, die Uni abschließen oder Ausbildungen abbrechen, neue Bundeskanzler wählen, krank werden. Ein paar Jünger sind ausgestiegen, neue dazugekommen, ein paar wenige Ältere sind gestorben. „Wir spielen", sagt Christian Stückl. „Nur wie, weiß keiner." Großveranstaltungen sind im Januar 2022 nur ohne Publikum erlaubt, aber bis Mai, hofft Stückl, wird das schon anders sein. Spielen sie halt in kleineren Gruppen oder vor weniger Zuschauern, man ist ja flexibel geworden. Christian Stückl ist ohnehin einer, den so schnell nichts umhaut, zumindest scheint es so. Er hat in den zwei Jahren vor allem mit Politikern über Kultur und Corona diskutiert und das neue Münchner Volkstheater eröffnet, das er wie nebenbei auch noch leitet. Ernsthaft Sorgen macht sich im Januar also niemand mehr. Das Schlimmstmögliche, sagen sie, das sei ja mit der Absage bereits passiert.

So sitzt Jesus-Spieler Frederik Mayet im März 2022 in der wiedereröffneten Passionskantine und beobachtet das Treiben im Raum: Maria und Maria Magdalena genehmigen sich einen Sekt, ein Henker bestellt eine Gulaschsuppe. Soweit, so passionsnormal. Nur sein ungeheuerliches Äußeres entlockt jedem, der reinkommt, mindestens einen Spruch. Mayet hat Augenringe, strähniges Haar, blutverschmierte Stirn. Es ist sein zweiter erster Tag im Jesus-Look. Mit großer Genauigkeit hat ihn die Maskenbildnerin in das buchstäbliche Leiden Christi verwandelt, ihn mit Dreck und Theaterblut eingeschmiert. In diesen Wochen entstehen wieder die aufwendigen Aufnahmen für den offiziellen Bildband. Unter seinem kratzigen roten Leinengewand trägt Mayet nur einen weißen Lendenschurz. Den muss er sich in einem speziellen Verfahren anlegen lassen, weil auch der Sicherheitsgurt für die Kreuzigung darin versteckt wird. Sich „windeln lassen" nennen er und sein Jesus-Kollege Rochus Rückel diese Prozedur. Dann wird Mayet über Lautsprecher gerufen und huscht auf die Bühne, fürs nächste Bild.

Immer mal wieder erinnert jemand daran, dass die Absage 2020 während dieser Foto-Aufnahmen kam. Als das symbolträchtige Datum überschritten ist, der 19. März, scheinen alle erleichtert. Es ist, als ob endlich das nächste Kapitel beginnt. Kein einziges Foto von damals haben sie behalten.

Jesus (Frederik Mayet) in seinem Kreuzigungs-Lendenschurz.

Jesus (Frederik Mayet) in his crucifixion-loincloth.

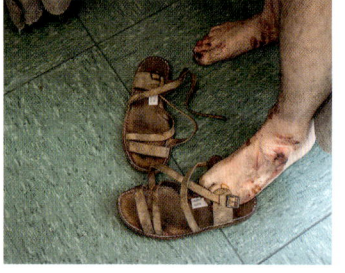

Von jetzt auf Jesus

Becoming Jesus

Der richtige Leidens-Look ist viel Arbeit: Frederik Mayet wird mit Kunstblut eingeschmiert (flüssig und stückig), mit Dreck eingerieben, er bekommt Augenringe verpasst und, natürlich, die Dornenkrone.

Creating the look of suffering is hard work: Frederik Mayet is smeared with artificial blood (liqud and lumpy) and dirt, he gets dark circles under his eyes and the crown of thorns, of course.

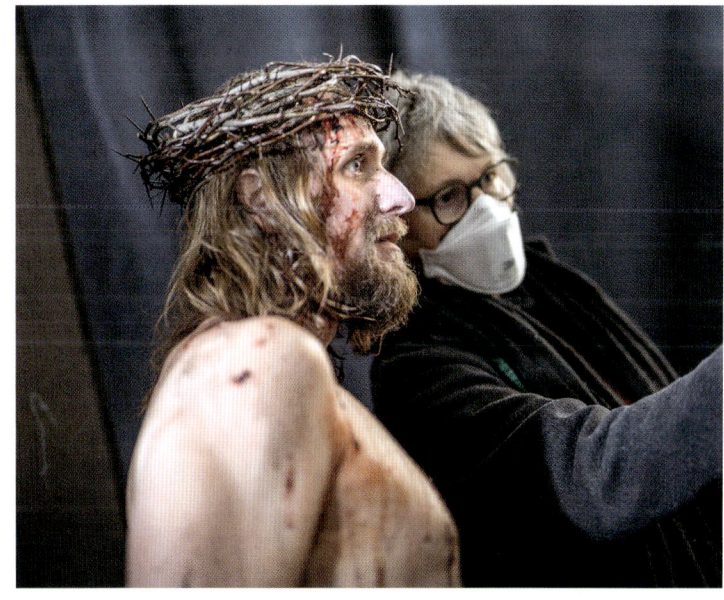

Scene 9:
The Women around Jesus

When Christian Stückl took over as director of the Passion Play, women who wanted to participate in the play had to be Catholic, unmarried, of course, and not older than 35 years. An odd consequence of this rule was, that many times Mary was younger than Jesus, her son. So, it's up to three brave women from Oberammergau to spend years protesting and fighting until finally, in 1990, the Bavarian Administrative Court in Munich grants the right to play to all women of Oberammergau – married or not, older, or younger than 35. And they also fight successfully to get a voice in the Passion Play Committee. Many men and a few women, too, don't agree with this at all. But their counterarguments sound absurd, even back then: after all, women did not take part in public life in Palestine 2000 years ago, and this being a historic play, they, unfortunately, must stay in the background. Moreover, not allowing married women to take part, is really meant as a protection for them, since it is hardly possible for a stressed-out mother and housewife to find the time for acting on top of everything else, right? Not to mention that Mary is supposed to be a virgin. The court, however, doesn't accept any of these arguments. When it comes to married Jesus actors, these rules are not taken too seriously either, after all.

Still, to this day, the Bible cannot really be called a feminist manifest, complex female figures are nowhere to be found. Next to countless large and important parts for men, there are three speaking parts for women in the Passion Play that are worth mentioning: Mary, Mary Magdalene and Veronica, who is one of the very few people to give Jesus comfort while he is carrying his cross by handing him a sweat towel. She only has three short lines. Christian Stückl has done a lot to make these parts more important and interesting, but more is always possible, says Mary actress Eva Reiser. Most things shown on stage lack historic evidence anyway, she says, so why not write some more meaningful lines for women. The other option, i.e., giving some of the male parts, like the disciples, or even the part of Jesus to women – it's still theatre, after all – is unthinkable for Stückl. That might be possible in professional theatre in Munich, but not in Oberammergau. Not yet.

Szene 9:
Die Jüngerinnen

Als Christian Stückl 1987 zum Spielleiter gewählt wird, ist er gerade mal 26. Das Dorf ist damals tief zerstritten über die Auslegung der Passion – über eine konservative oder eine sehr konservative. Oberammergau, das ist zu der Zeit noch frömmelndes Bauerntheater von Katholiken für andere Katholiken, künstlerisch nicht ernst zu nehmen. Man will die Tradition bewahren, indem man das Alte einfach immer weiter kopiert. Dass die Spiele durch Stückl immer offener und professioneller werden, das gefällt bis heute nicht jedem im Ort. Schon kurz nach seiner Wahl ging das los, damals schreiben ein paar Oberammergauer an seine Tür: „Totengräber von Ammergau, zieh Leine, sonst bekommst du nasse Beine." Hat ihn nicht beeindruckt.

Für die Frauen im Ort heißt das damals: Um mitmachen zu dürfen, müssen sie katholisch sein, klar, unverheiratet und nicht älter als 35. Was zur kuriosen Folge hat, dass Maria nicht selten jünger ist als Jesus, ihr Sohn. So liegt es an drei tapferen Oberammergauerinnen, jahrelang in eigener Sache zu protestieren, zu kämpfen und bis nach München zu ziehen, wo sie schließlich 1990 vor dem Verwaltungsgericht ein Spielrecht für alle Frauen erstreiten – auch für die verheirateten und über 35-jährigen. Und sie erstreiten auch ein Mitspracherecht im Passionsspielkomitee. Viele Männer und einige Frauen sind darüber alles andere als begeistert. Die Gegenargumente sind damals schon absurd: Frauen hätten im öffentlichen Leben vor 2000 Jahren in Palästina nun mal keine Rolle gespielt, und da dies ja ein historisches Spiel sei, müssen sie leider im Hintergrund bleiben. Außerdem sei das Spielverbot verheirateter Frauen auch zu deren Schutz da, denn wie soll eine gestresste Hausfrau und Mutter auch noch Theater spielen? Ganz zu schweigen von der angeblichen Jungfräulichkeit Marias. All das ließ das Gericht nicht gelten. Bei verheirateten Jesus-Darstellern nahm man es schließlich auch nicht so genau.

Dennoch ist die Bibel bis heute nicht gerade ein feministisches Manifest, kein Quell vielschichtiger Frauenfiguren. Drei erwähnenswerte Sprechrollen gibt es in der Passion, neben ungeheuer vielen Männerrollen: Maria, Maria Magdalena und Veronika, die Jesus als eine der Wenigen auf dem Kreuzweg Trost schenkt und ihm ihr Tuch reicht, aber gerade mal drei Sätzlein spricht. Christian Stückl bemüht sich, die Rollen etwas spannender zu machen, aber da ginge schon noch mehr, findet Maria-Darstellerin Eva Reiser. Historisch belegt sei doch ohnehin das Wenigste, also könne man den Frauen noch ein paar mehr sinnhaltige Sätze schreiben. Die andere Möglichkeit, einfach ein paar der Jünger oder gar Jesus mit einer Frau zu besetzen, – schließlich ist es immer noch Theater – ist für Stückl nicht vorstellbar. Das geht vielleicht am Profi-Theater in München, in Oberammergau geht es nicht. Noch nicht.

Frauen, in der Bibel eher unterrepräsentiert, sind auch bei den Spielern in der Unterzahl. Da ginge noch mehr, finden sie.
Andrea Hecht, Maria (rechts).

As in the Bible itself, women are also quite underrepresented in the Passion Play. More would be possible, they all agree.
Andrea Hecht, Mary (right).

Scene 10:
In the Name of the Church?

"I don't live a hundred percent according to the Bible," says Stückl. "But in a way, the story we tell on stage must be of some importance in your own life. For me, the text of the Passion Play goes far beyond any ordinary text in theatre." Stückl has no fear of contact with the Bible at all. Enthusiastically, he digs into the old stories, looks for values that have stood the test of time and thinks about Jesus as a social reformer.

Faith is one thing; the church is another. That's how the actors see it, too. Some of them are former altar boys who had their children baptized, others have left the church years ago or never were Christians at all, like for example the Muslims that take part in the play. Stückl himself grew up in a very Catholic environment, but ever since he became director of the Passion Play, he has had his problems with the church and has criticized it openly and publicly. He criticizes its growing distance to the people, its encrusted hierarchies, and lately also its failures and omissions concerning the clarification of the many cases of abuse.

Over many centuries, the Passion Play was a very Catholic, even pietistic play, directed by the local priest and inextricably linked to the church. Stückl, too, had to accept the advice, comments and criticism of the priest at first. Slowly but surely, however, he has managed to reduce the influence of the church. Today, the so-called "patronage agreement" which allowed the church to interfere with the casting procedure or individual scenes, does not exist anymore. All this doesn't mean, however, that he isn't more than happy to meet Catholic theologians to discuss and argue with them. In 2020, the actors of the Passion Play were officially invited to the Ash Wednesday Service in the Cathedral of Munich, the Frauenkirche. During the trip to Israel, they all pray together. Every cooperation with the church today is voluntary.

Working on the Passion Play does not make the actors and other participants any more or less religious. But they become more sensitive to a greater connection of things. And to the beauty of community. Those two things might be the same anyway. But Stückl isn't sure yet if there will be the traditional Lord's Prayer this year before every performance. "Probably yes. Doesn't bother anyone, after all."

Die Religion der Spieler ist mittlerweile egal, zweiter Spielleiter ist inzwischen ein Muslim: Abdullah Karaca (oben). Ein Fresko der katholischen Kirche Oberammergau (unten).

The religious confession of the actors does not matter anymore; the second director is a Muslim: Abdullah Karaca (above). A fresco in the Catholic church of Oberammergau (below).

Szene 10:
Im Namen der Kirche?

„Ich leb die Bibel nicht hundertprozentig", sagt Christian Stückl. „Aber auf eine Weise muss sich das, was wir auf der Bühne erzählen, im eigenen Leben schon widerspiegeln. Der Passionstext geht für mich über einen Theatertext hinaus." Stückl hat keinerlei Berührungsängste mit der Bibel, eifrig gräbt er sich hinein in die alten Geschichten, sucht nach Werten, die die Zeit überdauert haben und denkt über Jesus als Sozialreformer nach.

Glaube ist das eine, die Kirche etwas ganz anderes. So geht es auch den Spielern, von denen einige ehemalige Ministranten sind, ihre Kinder taufen lassen, andere längst aus der Kirche ausgetreten sind oder gar nie drin waren, wie die Muslime, die mitspielen. Stückl selbst ist sehr katholisch aufgewachsen, aber seit er Spielleiter ist, quält er sich mit der Kirche und kritisiert sie auch öffentlich. Dafür, dass sie sich von den Menschen entferne, dass sie hierarchisch verkrustet sei und in jüngster Zeit für die katastrophalen Versäumnisse bei der Aufklärung von Missbrauchsfällen, um nur ein paar Punkte zu nennen.

Über Jahrhunderte war die Passion ein katholisches, gar frömmelndes Spiel, geleitet vom Ortsgeistlichen, untrennbar mit der Kirche verbunden. Auch Stückl muss sich zu Beginn seiner Zeit als Spielleiter noch vom Ortspfarrer reinreden lassen. Nach und nach löst Stückl die Spiele jedoch aus dem Einfluss der Kirche. Auch den sogenannten „Patronatsvertrag", der der Kirche theoretisches Eingreifen in einzelne Szenen oder bei Besetzungen erlaubt hatte, gibt es inzwischen nicht mehr. Was nicht heißt, dass er sich nicht gern mit katholischen Theologen zum Streiten und Diskutieren trifft. Noch 2020 sind die Passionsspieler Gäste im Aschermittwochsgottesdienst in der Münchner Frauenkirche, auch auf der Reise nach Jerusalem finden gemeinsame Andachten statt. Jede Zusammenarbeit mit der Kirche basiert heute auf Freiwilligkeit.

Die Arbeit an der Passion macht auch die Spieler nicht mehr oder weniger religiös, aber doch empfänglicher für so etwas wie einen größeren Zusammenhang der Dinge. Oder die Schönheit von Gemeinschaft. Möglicherweise ist beides sowieso dasselbe. Ob es bei diesen Spielen 2022 aber wieder das traditionelle Vaterunser vor jeder Vorstellung geben soll, weiß Stückl noch nicht. „Wahrscheinlich schon", sagt er, „stört ja keinen."

Die Religion der Spieler ist mittlerweile egal. 2015 ernennt Stückl den muslimischen Regisseur Abdullah Karaca zum zweiten Spielleiter. Und damit zu einem potenziellen Nachfolger, auch wenn es im Grunde vollkommen unvorstellbar ist, dass überhaupt irgendjemand auf Christian Stückl nachfolgen kann.

Spirituell, ja, aber religiös? Nicht zwingend.
Eine Andacht in der St. Anna Kirche in Jerusalem.

*Spiritual, yes, but religious? Not necessarily.
A prayer in the St. Anne's church in Jerusalem.*

Scene 11:
Healing Wounds

He is not quite fit yet; just like so many others, Cengiz Görür has had Covid and had to skip several rehearsals. But now, he is leaning against a fence on a farm near the Passion Play Theatre and tries to pet Sancho, the passion play donkey. Together with two camels the animal is waiting here for his big day: he will carry the savior on stage. "He is so cute!" Görür says pulling out his mobile. Sancho remains unimpressed.

Der Hohepriester Kaiphas, hier gespielt von Andreas Richter, einem Jesus von 2010.

The High Priest Caiaphas, played by Andreas Richter, who was Jesus in 2010.

Görür has had two quite unsettling Covid years: In 2020 he dropped out of school and began studying at the Otto Falckenberg drama school in Munich. He commuted between the city and his hometown Oberammergau, had to get up very early and got home very late. His fellow students had lots of experience on stage – he didn't. He started skipping lessons, was unhappy, and finally dropped out. The past year he did various jobs like delivering pizza in Oberammergau. When you look at his face, it tells the story of the past two years. You can see it in all the players' faces, but especially in Görür's face; he is so young, was born in 2000 and is thus just 22 years old.

"It was unbelievable to see them all again," he says, his eyes beaming. Back in 2020, he often felt overwhelmed, he says, by the text, by the strange story and by his role as Judas. Now, he knows how to approach a role, how to understand even a character like Judas. After all, he has completed one-third of acting training and this is much more than all the others have to offer – despite all the professional approaches and the huge efforts put into it, the Passion Play is still mainly an amateur play. In the fall, Görür will start over at drama school, the school management has made an exception for him. You really have to look for them, but this forced pause did also have its positive sides, too.

In the spring of 2022 the actors are rehearsing every evening in the roofed open-air theatre, often until midnight and sometimes at temperatures just slightly above the freezing point. Monday outrage, Tuesday crucifixion, Wednesday resurrection. Things are getting serious.

The text of the Passion Play is difficult material. Mary says: "For the sake of my son, I will wish you peace, Jerusalem. For the sake of the Lord's temple, I will invoke happiness for you." So, who will invoke what and why, again? Luckily, Christian Stückl knows exactly how the lines should sound. He storms right through the scene and shows the actors how to play and how to say the words. He literally puts them into their mouths. He also tries to find images, to translate the abstract words into everyday language. He tells the despondent angel, for example, to pretend that he is speaking to his mother. He compares the Last Supper to a company event: "You must imagine that this is Jesus' motivation speech. The boss steps down and hands over the company to the disciples." And if none of that helps: "Try saying it in Bavarian!"

One evening shortly before Easter 2022, they are rehearsing "Bethany", a terribly lengthy scene as every-

Anton Preisinger Junior als Jünger Johannes und Eva Reiser als Maria.

Anton Preisinger junior as the disciple John and Eva Reiser, Mary.

Szene 11:
Heilende Wunden

Ganz stabil ist er noch nicht wieder, wie so viele andere hatte auch Cengiz Görür inzwischen Corona und musste mehrere Proben aussetzen. Aber jetzt steht er auf einem Bauernhof nahe des Passionstheaters an einem Zaun und streckt die Hand nach Sancho aus, seines Zeichens Passionsesel. Sancho wartet in Gesellschaft von zwei Kamelen auf seinen großen Tag: Er soll den Heiland auf die Bühne tragen. „So süß!", sagt Görür und zückt sein Handy. Sancho bleibt unbeeindruckt. Görür hat zwei verhältnismäßig aufregende Corona-Jahre hinter sich: 2020 brach er die Schule ab und ging an die Otto Falckenberg Schauspielschule nach München. Er pendelte zwischen Stadt und Dorf, spät heimkommen, früh aufstehen. Die anderen in seinem Jahrgang hatten so viel Theatererfahrung und er nicht. Er fing an zu schwänzen, war unglücklich, brach das Studium ab. Im vergangenen Jahr jobbte er als Pizzabote in Oberammergau. Die Zeit, die seit dem Haar- und Barterlass vergangen ist, sieht man ihm an. Man sieht sie allen an, vor allem aber den jungen: Cengiz Görür, geboren 2000, ist gerade einmal 22.

„Es war unglaublich, alle wieder zu treffen", sagt er strahlend. Bei der ersten Runde, damals, habe er sich oft überwältigt gefühlt vom Text, von dieser seltsamen Geschichte und dem Judas. Jetzt weiß er, wie man sich einer Rolle nähert, wie man auch einen wie den Judas verstehen kann. Ein Drittel Schauspielausbildung ist immerhin deutlich mehr, als die anderen vorzuweisen haben, die Passion ist bei all der Professionalisierung und dem enormen Aufwand noch immer ein Laienspiel. Im Herbst wird Görür noch mal neu starten an der Schauspielschule, die Schulleitung macht eine Ausnahme. Man muss zwar suchen, aber an manchen Stellen hat die Zwangspause auch etwas Gutes bewirkt.

Im Frühjahr 2022 probt die Truppe dann jeden Abend in dem überdachten Freilichttheater, oft bis Mitternacht, nicht selten bei Temperaturen um den Gefrierpunkt. Montag Empörung, Dienstag Kreuzigung, Mittwoch Auferstehung. Langsam wird es ernst.

Der Passionstext ist ein schwieriger Stoff. Maria sagt: „Um meines Sohnes willen will ich dir Frieden wünschen, Jerusalem, um des Tempels des Herrn willen,

Probenalltag mit echten Tieren.

Rehearsing with real animals.

one who is in it points out. So much standing around, so much saying goodbye. According to the New Testament, Bethany is the place near Jerusalem where Jesus raised Lazarus from the dead. The two Jesus actors are not allowed to use their textbooks anymore now, orders Stückl – it's getting serious. Frederik Mayet, dressed in his own clothes this time, is sitting in the audience area watching his fellow actor Rochus Rückel struggling through the words of the Sermon on the Mount. An eye for an eye, turn the other cheek, love thy neighbor. According to the Bible, the Sermon of the Mount was not held in Bethany at all, but – see above – working with the text is part of the poetic license.

"I think, I won't be on anymore today," one of the two Marys whispers, when Stückl allows a short break around 9:30 pm after they all have been waiting around in the cold theatre for more than two hours. "Go and get yourselves a cola," Stückl says. The rehearsal will take longer today. Something has changed in Oberammergau. The goal is within reach. Finally.

unseres Gottes, will ich dir Glück erflehen." Wer bitte will was warum erflehen? Zum Glück hat Christian Stückl eine genaue Vorstellung davon, wie die Sätze klingen sollen. Er stürmt mitten durch die Szene und spielt die Sätze vor, legt sie den Spielern buchstäblich in den Mund. Er versucht, Bilder zu finden, das Abstrakte ins Alltägliche zu übersetzen. Der verzagte Engel soll so tun, als spräche er mit seiner Mutter. Das letzte Abendmahl gleiche einer Firmenversammlung: „Ihr müsst euch vorstellen, das ist Jesus' Motivationsrede. Der Chef tritt ab und übergibt die Firma an die Jünger." Und wenn gar nichts hilft: „Sag's mal auf Bairisch!"

An einem Abend kurz vor Ostern 2022 steht „Bethanien" auf dem Plan, eine furchtbar längliche Szene, wie jeder betont, der darin mitspielt. So viel Herumstehen, so viele Abschiede. Laut Neuem Testament ist Bethanien der Ort nahe Jerusalem, an dem Jesus Lazarus von den Toten erweckte. Den beiden Jesus-Darstellern hat der Chef Textbuchverbot auf der Probe erteilt, es wird ernst. Frederik Mayet, diesmal wie alle wieder in Zivil, sitzt im Zuschauerraum und beobachtet seinen Kollegen Rochus Rückel, wie er sich durch Sätze der Bergpredigt kämpft. Aug um Aug, die andere Wange, die Nächsten lieben. Die Bergpredigt hielt Jesus zwar laut Bibel nicht in Bethanien, aber, siehe oben, mit dem Text zu arbeiten gehört zur künstlerischen Freiheit.

„Ich glaub, ich komm heut nicht mehr dran", raunt eine der zwei anwesenden Marias, als Stückl gegen halb zehn eine kurze Pause gestattet und sie schon zwei Stunden im kalten Theater gewartet hat. „Holt euch ein Spezi", sagt Stückl. Die Probe wird heute wieder länger dauern. Es hat sich etwas verändert in Oberammergau: Das Ziel ist in greifbare Nähe gerückt. Endlich und tatsächlich.

Aufnahmen für den aufwendig produzierten Foto-Bildband. Die Premiere rückt näher.

Working on the elaborately produced photo book. The premiere is getting closer.

Scene 12:
Stückl's Plan und God's Contribution

"If you want to make God laugh, tell him about your plans," Stückl says again and again. He doesn't really remember when he started using them, but these words by Blaise Pascal perfectly describe the events of the past two years – and they still fit now in 2022. The same day Russian troops are marching into Ukraine, Christian Stückl has a minor heart attack. Some say it was a warning shot, because he is constantly overtaxing himself. For a few moments everything is in danger again – a war, a director in the hospital. Unthinkable.

A few days later, however, at least Christian Stückl is released from the hospital. Rehab? No time. From one day to the next he quits smoking. From 80 cigarettes per day to zero. But he storms through the theatre as restlessly as ever. "I am still burning, just as I did before," he answers to the question if there isn't anything he plans to do differently now. "And if that means it's over faster, then that's how it is."

"Oh Lord, free the prisoners, be a spring of water for the thirsting and let us see your face in the night of death," the choir sings in the piece "Loss of Paradise" that accompanies the first living picture of the Passion Play. It tells the story of the expulsion from paradise, the very moment where the humans who have just been created experience pain and misery for the very first time. Maybe the world now isn't any better than it was in 2020. But maybe it's easier for us now to make compromises, easier too, to enjoy the good things of life since nothing can be taken for granted anymore. Maybe the world needs the Passion Play right now. And the people from Oberammergau are determined to put in on stage this year. They have suffered enough.

Szene 12:
Stückls Plan und Gottes Beitrag

„Wenn du Gott zum Lachen bringen willst, erzähl ihm von deinen Plänen", sagt Stückl immer wieder. Wann genau er damit angefangen hat, lässt sich schwer festmachen, aber natürlich passt dieser Spruch von Blaise Pascal hervorragend zu den vergangenen zwei Jahren und er passt auch noch 2022. An dem Tag im Februar, an dem russische Truppen in die Ukraine einmarschieren, erleidet Christian Stückl einen leichten Herzinfarkt. Ein Schuss vor den Bug, sagen manche, weil er sich so viel zumutet. Für ein paar Augenblicke ist wieder alles in Gefahr, ein Krieg, ein Spielleiter, der im Krankenhaus liegt. Nicht auszudenken.

Nach wenigen Tagen aber wird zumindest Christian Stückl wieder aus dem Krankenhaus entlassen. Reha? Keine Zeit. Von heute auf morgen hört er mit dem Rauchen auf. Vorher: achtzig Zigaretten am Tag, jetzt: null. Durch das Theater rennt er weiterhin so rastlos wie zuvor. „Ich brenn genauso weiter wie in der Vergangenheit", sagt er auf die Frage, ob er jetzt nicht irgendwas anders machen wolle. „Und wenn es dann schneller rum ist, ist es halt schneller rum."

„Herr, lass die Gebeugten aufrecht gehen, sei für die Dürstenden der Quell und lass in Todesnacht uns sehen dein Antlitz hell", heißt es im Chorstück „Der Verlust des Paradieses", passend zum ersten Lebenden Bild der Passion. Es erzählt von der Vertreibung aus dem Paradies, dem biblischen Moment, in dem die gerade erst erschaffenen Menschen zum ersten Mal Leid erfahren. Die Welt mag 2022 keinen Deut besser sein als 2020. Vielleicht aber ist der Mensch ja resilienter geworden, robuster, anpassungsfähiger. Den Bayern sagt man ja ohnehin eine gewisse Zähigkeit nach. Vielleicht ist aber auch die Bereitschaft zum Kompromiss größer geworden, oder die Fähigkeit, sich zu freuen, weil längst nichts mehr selbstverständlich ist. Möglich, dass die Welt die Passion jetzt brauchen kann. Die Oberammergauer jedenfalls sind fest entschlossen, das Spiel auf die Bühne zu bringen. Sie haben genug gelitten.

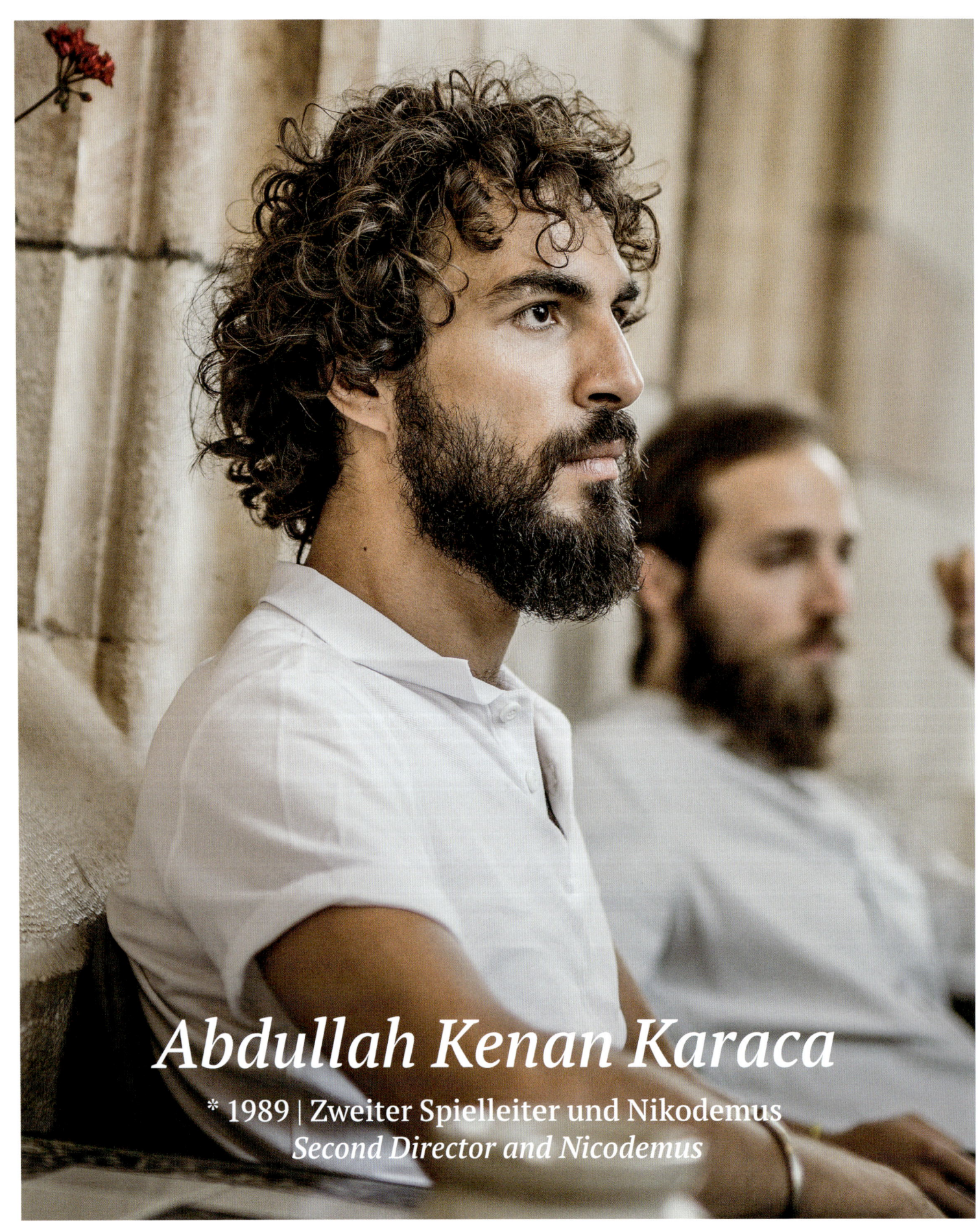

Abdullah Kenan Karaca
*1989 | Zweiter Spielleiter und Nikodemus
Second Director and Nicodemus

How does it feel to be on stage?
I am a theatre director, so for me, it feels very special. After all, I have had good reasons to decide not to become an actor. For me, it's quite strenuous trying not to constantly observe myself while I'm acting.

Who is Nicodemus?
Nicodemus is a Jewish priest; his name is mentioned in the Bible. He is not quite sure yet, what to think about Jesus, he doesn't know if he can believe him, but he tries to understand him. He can't get Jesus out of his mind. This internal struggle, this search for answers is something I can relate to.

You are also the second director. What does that mean?
That's hard to describe. I am not solely the dramatic advisor or solely the assistant director, I am also not really a deputy director. I just do what needs to be done. I attend all rehearsals, discuss new ideas with the director, and rewrite text passages.

Is the Passion Play spiritually important to you?
I am a Muslim, but I don't practice my religion very actively. Through the Passion Play I have learned a lot about Christianity and about Jesus, too. Who he was, what he wanted. The questions that come to my mind now during the Passion Play are more universal ones, e.g., what makes a good person? It's not Christian values that we show, but social values, how people should treat and approach each other.

What is your first memory of the Passion Play?
In 2000 I went to choir rehearsal like all my schoolmates; I knew the "Heil dir" by heart, the hymn of Oberammergau. Back then, I was the only boy with short hair, and I knew that, as a Muslim, I wouldn't be part of the play. But I must have sung well, because Christian Stückl came into my mother's tailor shop and convinced my parents to let me participate. I remember being on stage during the entry into Jerusalem: I really wanted to touch Jesus who was riding on the donkey. In 2010 I only sat in the audience area and felt like I was missing out on something great. I thought: "Next time, you must be part of this again, no matter what."

Will you be the director of the Passion Play in 2030?
I don't think about that right now.

Wie ist es, auf der Bühne zu stehen?
Ich bin Theaterregisseur, daher ist es schon sehr besonders. Ich hab mich ja aus gutem Grund mal dagegen entschieden, Schauspieler zu sein. Es kostet echt Anstrengung, dass ich mich nicht ständig selbst beim Spielen beobachte.

Wer ist Nikodemus?
Nikodemus ist ein jüdischer Priester, namentlich in der Bibel erwähnt. Er ist sich noch nicht ganz sicher, was er von Jesus halten soll, er weiß nicht, ob er ihm glauben soll, ringt aber um Verständnis für ihn. Jesus lässt ihn nicht los. Diesen Kampf, diese Suche nach Antworten kann ich gut nachfühlen.

Sie sind auch zweiter Spielleiter. Was bedeutet das?
Schwer zu sagen. Ich bin nicht nur Dramaturg oder nur Regieassistent, auch nicht unbedingt der Stellvertreter des Spielleiters. Ich mache, was anfällt. Ich bin bei allen Proben dabei, tausche mich mit dem Spielleiter über Ideen aus, mache die Textfassungen.

Bedeutet Ihnen die Passion spirituell etwas?
Ich bin Moslem, aber kein streng praktizierender. Durch die Passion habe ich viel übers Christentum erfahren und natürlich über Jesus. Wer war er, was wollte er? Die Fragen, die sich mir jetzt bei der Passion stellen, etwa, was einen guten Menschen ausmacht, sind ja universell. Wir verhandeln keine christlichen, sondern viel mehr gesellschaftliche Werte, den menschlichen Umgang miteinander.

Was ist Ihre erste Erinnerung an die Passionsspiele?
2000 ging ich wie alle Kinder aus meiner Schule zur Gesangsprobe, ich konnte das „Heil dir" auswendig, die Hymne von Oberammergau. Ich hatte damals als einziger kurze Haare und wusste, dass ich da als Moslem nicht mitspiele. Ich glaube, ich habe gut gesungen, denn Christian Stückl zog in die Schneiderei meiner Mutter und hat meine Eltern überredet, dass ich mitspielen darf. Ich weiß noch, ich war beim Einzug dabei und wollte unbedingt Jesus berühren, der auf dem Esel ritt. 2010 saß ich nur im Zuschauerraum und hatte das Gefühl, etwas Gigantisches zu verpassen. Ich dachte: „Egal, was kommt, du musst wieder dabei sein beim nächsten Mal."

Werden Sie 2030 Leiter der Passionsspiele sein?
Darüber mache ich mir keine Gedanken.

What is your first memory of the Passion Play?
It was cold. I was barefoot and walking onto the stage holding my father's hand. Then I stepped on his feet. That was in 1990.

What do you do when there is no Passion Play?
I am an architect and I work for the municipality of Oberammergau. One of our projects was to renovate the cafeteria, to make it the heart of the Passion Play, where everyone meets. People eat something or wait for their scenes. We put in a wooden floor, installed nice lights and hung curtains to reduce the noise level a little bit when it's crowded. We used to have only benches in there, which was very inconvenient for the actors who had to climb over them with their long costumes.

Is there a Passion Play tradition in your family?
My whole family is part of the play. My dad is a member of the High Council, my mom and my two children will be in the crowd. My husband is a carpenter, and he plays one of the thieves who are crucified next to Jesus.

Is faith important to you?
I am a religious person and Catholic in a way, but at the moment I am struggling with the church.

Who is Veronica?
Veronica hands a sweat towel to Jesus. She has three, no, four lines to say in the play. She has one very short appearance. In the Bible, she isn't mentioned at all. So, I don't have to be in the theatre until the second part of the Passion Play, in the evening. "How your face is covered in blood and sweat." This sentence shows quite well, what Veronica stands for. She is courageous enough to fight her way to Jesus despite all the soldiers present around him. She wants to alleviate his suffering. We have changed this scene, so that she is the last person he meets before the crucifixion. After all, it's mainly women who go with him on his last journey.

Was ist Ihre erste Erinnerung an die Passion?
Es war kalt. Ich bin barfuß an der Hand meines Vaters auf die Bühne gezogen und bei ihm auf die Füße gestiegen. Das war 1990.

Was machen Sie, wenn keine Passion ist?
Ich bin Architektin und bei der Gemeinde angestellt. Wir haben zum Beispiel die Passions-Kantine neu hergerichtet, sie ist ein Herzstück der Passion, da treffen sich alle. Sie essen Würstel oder warten auf ihren Auftritt. Wir haben Holzboden gelegt, gemütlicheres Licht und Vorhänge aufgehängt, damit es nicht so hallt, wenn es laut zugeht. Bisher waren nur Bänke drin, was sehr unpraktisch war, wenn die Darsteller mit den langen Gewändern drübersteigen mussten.

Gibt es in Ihrer Familie eine Passions-Tradition?
Meine ganze Familie spielt mit. Der Papa ist im Hohen Rat, die Mama wird mit meinen beiden Kindern im Volk dabei sein. Mein Mann ist Schreiner, spielt einen der Schächer, die neben Jesus am Kreuz hängen.

Spielt der Glaube eine Rolle für Sie?
Ich bin ein gläubiger Mensch, katholisch irgendwie auch, aber ich tu mich zurzeit schwer mit der Kirche.

Wer ist Veronika?
Veronika ist die, die Jesus das Schweißtuch reicht. Sie hat drei, nein, sogar vier Sätze. Sie kommt aber nur einmal kurz vor, in der Bibel ja überhaupt nicht. Ich muss also erst zum zweiten Teil der Passion ins Theater, am Abend. „Wie ist Dein Gesicht von Blut und Schweiß bedeckt", das repräsentiert ganz gut, wofür Veronika steht. Sie hat den Mut, sich trotz des großen Aufgebots an Soldaten zu Jesus durchzukämpfen, weil sie sein Leiden mildern will. Wir haben die Szene so geändert, dass sie seine letzte Begegnung vor der Kreuzigung ist. Es sind ja vor allem Frauen, die ihn auf seinem letzten Weg begleiten.

Vom Gelübde zum Welttheater

From the Vow to World Theatre

How a vow in dark times has developed into a world-famous event. A short history of the Oberammergau Passion Play

Written by Hans Kratzer

Christus, dargestellt von Alois Lang, und seine Jünger beim letzten Abendmahl. Zur 300. Wiederkehr der ersten Aufführung des Oberammergauer Passionsspiels wurde 1934 eine Jubiläumsvorstellung inszeniert (S. 100/101). Der Stich des Malers Carl Emil Doepler zeigt die Oberammergauer Passionsbühne im Jahr 1860. Damals stand das Spiel „in seiner schönsten Blüte", wie der Dichter Ludwig Thoma fand (unten).

Christ, played by Alois Lang, and his disciples at the Last Supper. For the 300th anniversary of the Oberammergau Passion Play, a special performance was put on stage in 1934 (p. 100/101). The engraving by the painter Carl Emil Doepler shows the stage of the Oberammergau Passion Play in 1860. Back then, the poet Ludwig Thoma found it to be "in its finest form" (below).

If you are looking for the origins of the Passion Play in Oberammergau, it is best to start with the name Kaspar Schisler. As he was the one, according to the village chronicles, who brought the black death to Oberammergau in the middle of the Thirty Years' War. Schisler, a day laborer who had found work in another village far away, is said to have come home shortly before the Sunday of the parish fair. He managed, the chronicles say, to sneak past the guards who were supposed to prevent the plague from coming into the village. "On Monday after the parish fair, he was a dead man," it says in the "History of the Village of Oberammergau" that the priest Joseph Alois Daisenberger wrote in 1858. He continues that in the few weeks after the fair between September and late October 1633, 84 people from Oberammergau died of the plague.

More thorough investigations, however, reveal some inconsistencies: The name Schisler, for example, appears neither in the natal nor in the death registers of the 1630s. Moreover, the church records show only two deaths in October 1633, which contradicts the village chronicles. So, it can be assumed, that the plague had already broken out at an earlier point in time in Oberammergau. Between October 1632 and October 1633, the death registers document 84 deaths.

Be it as it may, the story is just too good. And 90 percent of the village population had survived the plague after all. A very good reason to be thankful. So, on October 27th in 1633, the local council made its famous vow, a "solemn promise to present the passion tragedy every ten years", as Daisenberger wrote. After this vow, the story goes, no locals died from the plague anymore, "although many of them still showed the signs of the black death on their bodies". In other towns, chapels and memorials were built to keep the plague away – Oberammergau got its Passion Play. Which was not at all uncommon in the 17th century; religious plays were very popular back then. The Passion Play of Oberammergau, however, has stood the test of time and has grown to be the most famous Passion Play in the world.

The very first Passion Play was held at Pentecost in 1634 in the graveyard next to the parish church. The text and dramatic composition were taken from older passion play versions, like for example from the Passion-"Tragedi" printed in Augsburg in 1566. For the church historian Manfred Eder this mix of "a Meistersinger drama rooted in Protestantism and a medieval Catholic people's play" was unbalanced and in disequilibrium right from the beginning. And so, it took a while until the quality of the play improved. In the prologue of the text

Außenansicht des damals umgestalteten Theaters mit seiner Neorenaissance-Fassade. Eine Fotografie aus dem Jahr 1893.

External view of the then newly renovated theatre with its Neo-Renaissance façade. A photo from 1893.

Wie aus einem Gelübde in finsteren Zeiten ein weltberühmtes Spektakel wurde. Eine kleine Geschichte der Oberammergauer Passionsspiele

Von Hans Kratzer

Sucht man nach den Ursprüngen der Oberammergauer Passion, fängt man am besten mit dem Namen Kaspar Schisler an. Der nämlich, so heißt es in einer alten Dorfchronik, habe mitten im Dreißigjährigen Krieg die Pest nach Oberammergau gebracht. Der Tagelöhner Schisler, der sich in der Fremde verdingt hatte, soll kurz vor dem Kirchweihfest heimgekehrt und sich heimlich an den Wachposten vorbeigeschlichen haben, die damals das Einschleppen der Pest verhindern sollten. „Schon am Montage nach der Kirchweih war er eine Leiche", heißt es in der „Geschichte des Dorfes Oberammergau", die der Pfarrer Joseph Alois Daisenberger 1858 verfasst hat. In wenigen Wochen, von September bis Ende Oktober 1633, seien danach 84 Oberammergauer hinweggerafft worden.

Bei genauen Nachforschungen aber gibt es Ungereimtheiten: So ist der Name Schisler in den 1630er-Jahren weder im Geburts- noch im Sterberegister dokumentiert. Überdies sind in den Kirchenbüchern im Oktober 1633 lediglich zwei Sterbefälle eingetragen, was gegen die Behauptung der Dorfchronik spricht. Es liegt also nahe, dass die Pest in Oberammergau bereits früher ausgebrochen ist. Von Oktober 1632 bis Oktober 1633 weist das Sterbebuch tatsächlich 84 Gestorbene aus.

Sei's drum, die Geschichte ist einfach zu gut, zudem hatten ja 90 Prozent der Bevölkerung die Pest überlebt. Grund genug für Dankbarkeit. Also legte der Gemeindevorstand am 27. Oktober 1633 das berühmte Gelübde ab, ein „Verlobniß, die Passionstragödie alle zehn Jahre zu halten", wie es Daisenberger formulierte. Daraufhin soll kein Einheimischer mehr an der Pest gestorben sein, „obwohl noch etliche die Pestzeichen an sich hatten". Während anderswo Pestkapellen und Pestsäulen errichtet wurden, bekam Oberammergau auf diese Weise ein Passionsspiel. Das war im 17. Jahrhundert keinesfalls ungewöhnlich, religiöse Schauspiele erfreuten sich damals einer großen Popularität. Die Oberammergauer Darstellung des Leidens und Sterbens Jesu Christi aber überdauerte die Zeiten und wuchs zum weltweit bekanntesten Passionsspiel überhaupt heran.

Die erste Aufführung fand am Pfingstfest des Jahres 1634 auf dem Gottesacker neben der Pfarrkirche statt. Text und Dramaturgie entnahmen die Oberammergauer aus älteren Vorlagen, etwa aus einer 1566 gedruckten Augsburger Passions-„Tragedi". Für den Kirchenhistoriker Manfred Eder trug dieser Mischmasch „aus einem protestantisch getönten Meistersingerdrama und einem katholisch geprägten mittelalterlichen Volksspiel" von Anfang an allerdings etwas Unausgeglichenes in sich. So dauerte es eine Weile, bis sich die Qualität des Spiels ver-

Zeichnerische Darstellung der Oberammergauer Passionsspiele mit Publikum aus der Zeit um 1840. Damals verfasste ein Kaufmann den ersten Bericht in englischer Sprache.

Drawing of the Oberammergau Passion Play with an audience from around 1840. In those days, a merchant wrote the first review about the play in English.

version of 1662, the narrator asked the audience to be lenient if they noticed any mistakes, as the players were only "ordinary farmers". 70 years later, it was even decided to shorten some scenes, as the director Max Anton Erlböck wrote: "this prattle ... has taken much too long for the people."

After the agreement was reached in 1680 that the Passion Play would from now on be held in the years with the digit zero at the end, the Passion Play soon was subject to political pressure. As he suspected greed and abuse, Kurfürst Max III Joseph prohibited all passion plays in Bavaria on March 31st, 1770. His justification: "The greatest secret of our holy religion does not belong on stage." In later years as well, the people from Oberammergau were not always able to keep their vow. During the secularization years (1803), countless monasteries were dissolved, and the presentation of the Passion Play was prohibited once again. In 1920, shortly after World War I, and in 1940 during World War II the plays were canceled due to the adverse circumstances. And in 2020, the play had to be postponed because of the Covid pandemic.

The Passion Play of 1850 – a ceaseless stream of music, colors, and movements

At the end of the 19th century, visitor figures shot up, which was on the one hand due to the relocation of the play to the "passion meadow", where the Passion Play Theatre stands today. The other and more important reason was the improved rail connection. Before the train came, the journey from Munich to Oberammergau by horse bus had taken at least two days. The records of Anna Mary Howitt, a British art student who travelled from Munich to Oberammergau in a horse-drawn carriage in July 1850 give a nice impression of the time. "You feel dizzy and exhausted from the ceaseless stream of music, color, and movement," she wrote enthusiastically after her visit to the Passion Play. She couldn't imagine, however, how the local viewers could bear the scorching sun on their heads for eight hours straight, "not to mention the pressing closeness in their seats". She herself sat in a box, but even there, she wrote, the viewers soon seemed pale and weary.

besserte. Im Prolog des Textes von 1662 bat der Sprecher noch alle um Nachsicht bei etwaigen Fehlern, denn sie seien nur „grobe paurs leith". 70 Jahre später sah man sich gar gezwungen, manche Szenen zu kürzen, da nach den Worten des Frühmessers Max Anton Erlböck „dises geschwäz ... den leuthen vihl zu lang gewest ..."

Nachdem man sich 1680 darauf geeinigt hatte, fortan in den Jahren mit einer runden Zehnerzahl zu spielen, geriet die Passion alsbald unter politischen Druck. Gewinnsucht und Missbrauch witternd, erließ Kurfürst Max III. Joseph am 31. März 1770 ein Generalverbot für sämtliche Passionsspiele in Bayern. Die Begründung: „Das größte Geheimnis unserer heiligen Religion gehört nicht auf die Schaubühne." Auch später konnten die Oberammergauer ihr Gelübde nicht immer erfüllen. In der Zeit der Säkularisation (1803) wurden nicht nur viele Klöster aufgehoben, sondern auch die Aufführung der Passion verboten. Den widrigen Zeitumständen fielen zudem die Spiele im Nachkriegsjahr 1920 sowie im Kriegsjahr 1940 zum Opfer. Die Passionsspiele 2020 wurden wegen der Corona-Pandemie verschoben.

Das Passionsspiel von 1850 – ein ununterbrochener Strom von Musik, Farben und Bewegungen

Am Ende des 19. Jahrhunderts schnellten die Besucherzahlen in die Höhe, was zum einen der Verlegung des Spielorts auf die „Passionswiese", dem Platz des heutigen Passionstheaters, geschuldet war, mehr noch aber der ausgebauten Bahnanbindung. Vorher hatte eine Reise per Pferdeomnibus von München nach Oberammergau mindestens zwei Tage gedauert. Einen erhellenden Einblick in jene Zeit gewähren die Aufzeichnungen der englischen Kunststudentin Anna Mary Howitt, die im Juli 1850 mit dem Stellwagen von München aus anreiste, übernachtet wurde in Murnau. „Man fühlte sich ganz schwindelig und erschöpft von dem ununterbrochenen Strom von Musik, Farben und Bewegungen", schwärmte sie nach dem Besuch des Passionsspiels. Wie die Landleute die sengende Julisonne acht Stunden lang auf ihren Köpfen ertragen konnten, das blieb ihr allerdings unvorstellbar, „ganz zu schweigen von der drangvollen Enge auf ihren Plätzen". Sie selbst saß geschützt in einer Loge, aber auch dort wirkten, wie sie schreibt, bald alle Gäste blass und ermattet.

In jener Zeit setzte der Aufschwung des Tourismus ein. Je mehr ausländische Magazine über das Passionsspiel berichteten, desto mehr Prominenz machte sich auf

Die Gäste, die im Mai und Juni 1922 zu den Passionsspielen nach Oberammergau reisten, wurden von Kindern in Empfang genommen. Diese hielten Schilder mit den Namen der Unterkünfte in die Höhe (oben).
Mit Hut und Mantel: Besucher der Passionsspiele von 1922 genießen die Mittagspause auf einer Dorfwiese (unten).

The guests who had traveled to Oberammergau in May and June 1922 to see the Passion Play were welcomed by children. These held up signs with the names of the accommodations (above). Visitors of the Passion Play 1922 – all in coats and hats – enjoy the lunch break on a village meadow (below).

Ankunft von mit Koffern beladenen Gästen im Festspieljahr 1930. Die Zuschauerhalle wurde damals auf 5200 Plätze erweitert (oben). Kardinal Michael von Faulhaber nahm 1930 die Weihe der neuen Festspielhalle vor (Mitte). Im August 1930 sah der amerikanische Automagnat Henry Ford die umjubelte Neuinszenierung des Passionsspiels. Hier im Gespräch mit dem Christusdarsteller Anton Lang (unten). Das Passionstheater in einer Aufnahme um das Jahr 1925. Die am Straßenrand geparkten Autos tragen Kennzeichen aus München und Oberbayern (rechts).

Guests arriving with their luggage in the Passion Play year 1930. Back then, the audience hall was increased to hold 5,200 seats (above). Cardinal Michael von Faulhaber consecrated the new Passion Play Hall in 1930 (Center). In August 1930, the American automobile magnate Henry Ford saw the highly acclaimed new staging of the Passion Play. Here, he is talking to Jesus actor Anton Lang (below). A photograph of the Passion Play Theatre from around 1925. The cars parked at the roadside have license plates from Munich and Upper Bavaria (right).

In those days, tourism became more and more important in the region. The more foreign newspapers wrote about the Passion Play, the more VIPs found their way to the Ammertal valley. Clemens Brentano in 1840, Hans Christian Andersen in 1860, King Ludwig II in 1870, Thomas Alva Edison in 1890, Gustave Eiffel in 1900. Writers, aristocrats and intellectuals mingled freely with loudly praying pilgrims. By then, the regional event had been caught up in the maelstrom of secular globalization, and the town had to face the question of how to continue with it. During this phase of affirmation around 1860, the village priest Joseph Alois Daisenberger rewrote the Passion Plays text to make it more vivid and figurative and the play more traditional. This impressed the Bavarian poet Ludwig Thoma who saw the play "in its finest form", which it lost again later, according to Thoma, due to "unhealthy speculations and hopes of excessive and easy profits".

For the Passion Play 1880, the London travel agencies Henry Gaze and Thomas Cook already sold package deals including round-trip travel tickets, an overnight stay, and the theatre ticket. Back then, more than 100,000 visitors came; 20 years later, however, the number had gone up to 175,000 guests. And the growing success brought growing demands: costumes, sets, and technical equipment became more sophisticated; a theatre for today 4,400 viewers was built – to date the largest open-air stage with a roofed audience area in the world. And the number of participants grew as well. While only 60 to 70 people took part in the play in 1634, this number has gone up to over 2,000 today.

den Weg ins Ammertal: 1840 Clemens Brentano, 1860 Hans Christian Andersen, 1870 König Ludwig II., 1890 Thomas Alva Edison, 1900 Gustave Eiffel. Literaten, Adlige und Intellektuelle mischten sich munter mit laut betenden Pilgern. Spätestens jetzt, da das regionale Ereignis Passion vom Sog der säkularen Globalisierung erfasst wurde, stand das Dorf vor der Frage, wie es weitergehen sollte. In dieser Phase der Selbstvergewisserung um 1860 verpasste der Ortspfarrer Joseph Alois Daisenberger dem Text eine bildhaftere Sprache und dem Geschehen mehr Volkstümlichkeit. Davon beeindruckt, fand der Dichter Ludwig Thoma das Spiel nun „in seiner schönsten Blüte" und in einer Eigenart, die es später unter dem Einfluss von „ungesunden Spekulationen und von Hoffnungen auf unmäßigen und leichten Gewinn" verloren habe.

Für das Passionsspiel von 1880 verkauften die Londoner Reisebüros Henry Gaze und Thomas Cook bereits Pauschal-Arrangements, die Hin- und Rückreise, Übernachtung sowie die Eintrittskarte beinhalteten. Wurden seinerzeit mehr als 100 000 Besucher gezählt, erschienen 20 Jahre später bereits 175 000 Gäste. Mit dem Erfolg wuchsen die Ansprüche. Kulissen, Kostüme und Technik wurden üppiger, man baute ein Theater für 4400 Zuschauer, die bis heute weltweit größte Freiluftbühne mit überdachtem Zuschauerraum. Auch die Schar der Mitwirkenden wuchs. Waren es 1634 noch 60 bis 70 Spielerinnen und Spieler, sind es heute mehr als 2000.

Omnibusse und Autos – 1922 eine Seltenheit in Oberammergau – füllten die Straßen mit Lärm und Abgasen

Dass die Oberammergauer in den 1920er-Jahren ein lukratives Filmangebot aus Hollywood ablehnten, war vermutlich kein Schaden. Wer die Passion erleben wollte, musste schon in die bayerische Bergwelt reisen. Internationales Flair war trotzdem zu spüren: „Omnibusse und Autos – damals eine Seltenheit in Oberammergau – füllten die engen Straßen mit Lärm und ungewohnten Abgasen", erinnerte sich später der gebürtige Oberammergauer Ernst Maria Lang an das Passionsspiel von 1922. Auf den Wiesen landeten Flugzeuge von Junkers. Allerorten wurde Englisch gesprochen. Der Ort war hin- und hergerissen zwischen dem Beharren auf der konservativ-katholischen Werteordnung und einem

Das Passionstheater während der Premierenvorstellung des Sonderspiels im Jahr 1934. Die Nationalsozialisten begannen damals Einfluss auf das Spiel zu nehmen.

The Passion Play Theatre during the premiere of the anniversary year 1934. Back then, the National Socialists began to influence the play.

Busses and cars – a very rare sight in Oberammergau in 1922 – filled the streets with their noises and strange exhaust fumes

The decision of the town to turn down an attractive movie offering from Hollywood in the 1920s, was probably not a bad one. Those who wanted to see the Passion Play, just had to come to the Bavarian Alps. But you could still feel the international flair: "Busses and cars – very rare back then in Oberammergau – filled the narrow streets with their noises and strange exhaust fumes," Ernst Maria Lang from Oberammergau remembers later about the Passion Play of 1922. Junker airplanes landed on the meadows; many people spoke English. The town was torn between preserving the conservative Catholic values and living modern laicism. The arrogant tendencies coming with the latter are well reflected in the comments of Bavarian author Lion Feuchtwanger: "They are dreadful as soon as they open their mouths. Not a trace of a spirit to be found." In August 1930, the American automobile magnate Henry Ford saw the highly acclaimed new staging of play director Georg Johann Lang. Out of appreciation, Ford wanted to give Lang a car, but he denied it with a smile. Ernst Maria Lang wrote down his father's answer to Ford: "Mr. Ford, I am very honored by your offer, but I don't need a car. And should I ever need one, I will buy it myself." In the anniversary of 1934, Jean-Paul Sartre and Simone de Beauvoir were among the audience – and absolutely thrilled. It was another visitor, however, who was the center of attention that year: Adolf Hitler. When he came out on the balcony of his hotel during the lunch break, the masses cheered on him hysterically. As a commemorative present, he received a photo album with dedication: "To our Führer, the protector of German cultural heritage, from the Passion Play village Oberammergau." His father, too, was urged to join the National Socialist Party, writes Ernst Maria Lang. And he did, not because he supported their ideas, but because he worried about his Passion Play. This had developed a noticeably new tone, as the New York Times wrote. It is not easy to understand, who did and believed what back then based on which motives.

modernen Laizismus, dessen Hang zum Hochmut sich im Urteil des Autors Lion Feuchtwanger über die Spiele widerspiegelt: „Fürchterlich werden sie, wenn sie den Mund auftun ... Man findet nicht die Spur von einem Geist."

Im August 1930 sah der amerikanische Automagnat Henry Ford die umjubelte Neuinszenierung des Spielleiters Georg Johann Lang. Ford wollte Lang in Anerkennung ein Auto schenken, was jener aber lächelnd ablehnte. Ernst Maria Lang notierte die Erwiderung seines Vaters: „Mr. Ford, Ihr Angebot ehrt mich sehr, aber ich brauche kein Auto. Und sollte ich doch einmal eines benötigen, dann kaufe ich mir das selber."

Es ist nicht leicht zu durchschauen, wer in der Nazizeit aus welchen Motiven welchen Überzeugungen anhing

1934 bei den Jubiläumsspielen waren unter den Besuchern auch Jean-Paul Sartre und Simone de Beauvoir, sie zeigten sich hellauf begeistert. Im Mittelpunkt aber stand damals ein anderer: Adolf Hitler. Als er sich in der Mittagspause auf dem Balkon des Hotels zeigte, huldigte ihm eine hysterisch schreiende Menge. Als Erinnerungsgeschenk erhielt er ein Fotoalbum mit Widmung: „Unserem Führer, dem Schützer deutschen Kulturgutes, vom Passionsdorf Oberammergau."

Auch seinem Vater, so schreibt Ernst Maria Lang, sei der Eintritt in die Partei angetragen worden. Nicht aus Überzeugung habe er es getan, sondern aus Sorge um sein Passionsspiel, dem man, wie die New York Times schrieb, einen neuen Tonfall anmerkte. Nie sei der jüdische Pöbel in Oberammergau gewalttätiger gewesen. Es ist nicht leicht zu durchschauen, wer damals aus welchen Motiven welchen Überzeugungen anhing. Jedenfalls standen die Passionsspiele von 1934 unter dem Schutz der Nazi-Regierung. 1942 sagte Hitler, allein schon um das Bewusstsein der jüdischen Gefahr wach zu halten, müssten die Oberammergauer Passionsspiele unbedingt erhalten werden.

Als das zurecht umstrittenste Passionsspiel-Thema erwies sich die Darstellung der Juden. Schon 1880 gab es Beschwerden wegen der groben Zeichnung der Juden als blutrünstige Christus-Mörder, während Statthalter Pilatus stets als der edle Römer gezeigt worden sei. Der damalige Bürgermeister Raimund Lang sagte bei einer Gemeinderatssitzung im März 1939, die Passion sei „das antisemitischste Spiel, das wir überhaupt kennen". Sogar nach 1945 schwelte der Antijudaismus weiter, noch 1950 und 1960 wurde völlig unreflektiert ein Jesus-Darsteller gewählt, der mit den Nazis sympathisiert hatte. Nach dem Zweiten Vatikanischen Konzil in den 60er-Jahren, bei dem sich die Kirche zu der Erklärung durchgerungen hatte, die Juden seien nicht für den Tod Jesu verantwortlich, musste der Vatikan die Oberammergauer auffordern, ihr Spiel zu erneuern. Doch das Dorf zeigte sich widerwillig. In Amerika riefen jüdische

Als Reichskanzler Adolf Hitler am 13. August 1934 mit einer großen Entourage von Nazigrößen die Jubiläums-Passionsspiele besuchte, huldigte ihm eine hysterisch schreiende Menge.

When Reich Chancellor Adolf Hitler visited the Passion Play on August 13, 1934, accompanied by a large group of Nazi leaders, a hysterical crowd cheered on him.

VOM GELÜBDE ZUM WELTTHEATER

Mit dem wachsenden Tourismus ging eine große Nachfrage nach Oberammergauer Holzschnitzkunst einher. Christus-, Heiligen- und Engelsfiguren sowie Krippen und sonstige Andenken bescherten dem Ort gute Einkünfte.

The growing tourism also brought an increasing demand for Oberammergau woodcarvings. Carved figures of Christ, saints, and angels as well as nativity scenes and other souvenirs brought the town substantial additional income.

At any rate, the Passion Play of 1934 was under the Protection of the Nazi government. In 1942 Hitler said that the Oberammergau Passion Play definitely had to be preserved to keep the awareness of the Jewish danger alive. The presentation of the Jews in the Passion Play has justly proved to be the most disputed subject in the history of the play. As early as in 1880 there were complaints because of the very rude presentation of the Jews as the bloodthirsty murderers of Christ, while Governor Pontius Pilate was shown as a noble Roman. The then-mayor, Raimund Lang, said during a meeting of the local council in March 1939, that the Passion Play was "the most antisemitic play we know". And even after 1945 Anti-Judaism was still tangible in the play. Without any reflection, a Jesus actor was chosen in 1950 and 1960, who had sympathized with the Nazis. After the Second Vatican Council in the 1960s, where the church had finally brought itself to officially declare that the Jews were not responsible for the death of Jesus, it was Vatican officials that had to urge the people of Oberammergau to renew their play. The town, however, was still reluctant. Jewish organizations in the USA called for a boycott of the 1970 Passion Play and Cardinal Döpfner withdrew the "Missio Canonica", the mission order of the Catholic church. Finally, the locals started thinking.

In 1980, there was a violent dispute about the text of the Passion Play. On the one hand, there was the so-called "Passio nova" written by the Benedictine monk Ferdinand Rosner in 1750, which was put on stage in many Bavarian villages. In a public survey, however, 75 percent of the locals voted against the well-known Rosner version. So, the organizers stuck to the traditional text, which had been reworked in 1850 by Joseph Daisenberger and which was still criticized by some as antisemitic. The battle lines between traditionalists and reformers were even separating entire families.

After the 350th anniversary of the Passion Play, celebrated in 1984, the organizers faced a crucial decision. The question of whether to stick to tradition without any changes became more and more pressing, as this could bear the risk of losing international recognition. This pressure paved the way for real renewal. In 1987 the then only 26-year-old Christian Stückl was elected director by the local council – with a narrow minority. He immediately forged ahead with modernizations, although he was harshly criticized by the traditionalists.

The era Stückl – he first directed the Passion Play in 1990 – brought the great renewal: emancipation from the church, a confrontation with the antisemitism in the play and the text; and he chose a protestant for one of the main parts for the very first time. Married women and women older than 35 were also allowed to participate for the first time in 1990 – a right they had fought for themselves in court. Some traditionalists, such as the local priest Franz Dietl saw these developments as dangerous and even the end of the world coming.

Stückl didn't let himself be put off, however, and asked Stefan Hageneier, a professional stage and costume designer, to work with him. Markus Zwink, the musical director, is a master of his craft, too. Those three have made the play more and more professional.

And moreover, Stückl has managed to get many young locals enthusiastic about the play again – many of whom had turned their backs on the pietistic event. By now, the religious confession of the participants doesn't matter anymore, faith is not the most important thing. In July 2015, the local council elected the Muslim theatre director Abdullah Kenan Karaca as the second director of the Passion Play. Maybe he will be the one to follow in Stückl's footsteps one day?

Organisationen vor der Passion 1970 gar zum Boykott der Spiele auf und Kardinal Döpfner entzog den Spielen die „Missio Canonica", den kirchlichen Sendungsauftrag. So langsam regte sich was in Oberammergau.

1980 entbrannte dann ein Streit um den Passionstext. Zur Debatte stand die sogenannte „Passio nova" aus der Feder des Ettaler Benediktiners Ferdinand Rosner von 1750, die in vielen Passionsspielorten aufgeführt wurde. Bei einer Bürgerbefragung sprachen sich jedoch Dreiviertel der Oberammergauer gegen die anerkannte Rosner-Inszenierung aus. Man hielt an dem 1850 von Joseph Daisenberger überarbeiteten Text fest, den manche weiterhin als antisemitisch kritisierten. Quer durch die Familien verliefen die Fronten des Streits zwischen Traditionalisten und Reformern.

Nach der 1984 begangenen 350-Jahr-Feier standen die Passionsspiele dann an einem Scheidepunkt. Immer dringlicher wurde die Frage, ob man uneingeschränkt an der Tradition festhalten wollte – auf die Gefahr hin, weltweit Zuspruch zu verlieren. Unter diesem Druck wurden die Weichen auf Neuerung gestellt. Der Gemeinderat wählte 1987 mit knapper Mehrheit den erst 26-jährigen Christian Stückl zum Spielleiter, der die Modernisierung sogleich vorantrieb, obwohl er von den Traditionalisten heftig angefeindet wurde.

Mit der Ära Stückl, der die Passion 1990 zum ersten Mal inszenierte, begann die große Erneuerung: eine Emanzipation von der Kirche, eine Auseinandersetzung mit dem Antisemitismus in Spiel und dem Text, es gab einen ersten protestantischen Hauptdarsteller. Auch verheiratete Frauen und jene, die älter waren als 35, durften 1990 erstmalig mitspielen, was sie sich allerdings selbst vor Gericht erstritten hatten. Manche wie der Ortspfarrer Franz Dietl sahen gefährliche Entwicklungen, ja sogar den Weltuntergang heraufziehen.

Der Spielleiter ließ sich nicht beirren und holte mit Stefan Hageneier einen professionellen Bühnen- und Kostümbildner an seine Seite, Markus Zwink, der musikalische Leiter, ist ebenfalls Meister seines Fachs. Das Trio professionalisierte das Laienspiel immer mehr. Überdies gelang es Stückl, viele junge Oberammergauer, die sich vom einst frömmelnden Spiel abgewendet hatten, wieder für die Passion zu begeistern. Inzwischen spielt die Religion der Mitwirkenden keine Rolle mehr, der Glaube steht nicht im Vordergrund. Im Juni 2015 bestimmte der Gemeinderat den muslimischen Regisseur Abdullah Kenan Karaca zum zweiten Leiter der Passionsspiele. Ob er es sein wird, der eines Tages Christian Stückls großes Erbe antreten wird?

Die Frauenfiguren Maria und Maria Magdalena, ausdrucksstark gespielt von Anni Rutz und Klara Mayr, bei den Jubiläumsspielen 1934. Zum „Schutz gegen die Überfremdung" erließ das Passionskomitee damals strengere Mitwirkungsbestimmungen.

The female figures Mary and Mary Magdalene, expressively played by Anni Rutz and Klara Mayr, in the anniversary Passion Play of 1934. As a "protection against foreign infiltration", the Passion Committee introduced stringent participation provisions that year.

Gabriele Weinfurter-Zwink
* 1957 | Altistin im Passionschor
Contralto in the Passion Play Choir

What do you do when there is no Passion Play?
I am a full-time soprano singer at the Bavarian Radio Choir.

How did you end up in Oberammergau?
I was born in Munich and have lived in Oberammergau since 1987. My husband is Markus Zwink, the musical director of the Passion Play. His whole family is a Passion Play family – his father was the understudy for Jesus and second director, and his mother was an alto soloist and would have played the role of Mary hadn't she been married. In the beginning, it was difficult here. People are open to strangers when it's about art, but when you are from too far away, they are also reserved. It got better when I took over the children's choir in town.

What is the most beautiful music piece in the Passion Play?
The compositions of my husband, of course. But I get goosebumps when I hear the "Entry into Jerusalem". That's a brilliant piece by composer Rochus Dedler. It's so well done emotionally. When after several minutes of introductory music, the choir sets in with "Heil dir, oh Davids Sohn" (Hail, oh Son of David)", that's incredible.

What's going on in your family during the Passion Play?
Very crazy: My husband conducts, I sing alto, my two grown-up daughters sing soprano, and one of them also assists my husband. I am really happy to be on stage with my daughters and to be able to sing a duet with them.

Was machen Sie, wenn keine Passion ist?
Ich singe hauptberuflich im Chor des Bayerischen Rundfunks als Sopranistin.

Wie sind Sie in Oberammergau gelandet?
Ich bin Münchnerin und lebe erst seit 1987 in Oberammergau. Mein Mann ist der musikalische Leiter der Passionsspiele Markus Zwink, seine Familie ist also die Passionsfamilie – sein Vater war Ersatz-Christus und zweiter Spielleiter, die Mutter Altsolistin und wäre Maria geworden, wenn sie nicht verheiratet worden wäre. Der Anfang hier war schwierig, man ist Fremdem gegenüber aufgeschlossen, wenn's um Kunst geht, aber auch verschlossen, wenn jemand von ganz woanders kommt. Als ich den Kinderchor hier im Dorf übernommen habe, wurde es besser.

Welches ist das schönste Musikstück der Passion?
Die Kompositionen meines Mannes, klar. Aber Gänsehaut bekomme ich beim „Einzug nach Jerusalem", das ist ein genialer Wurf des Komponisten Rochus Dedler. Das ist emotional so gut gemacht. Wenn beim „Einzug nach Jerusalem" nach mehreren Minuten der Chor „Heil dir, oh Davids Sohn" einsetzt, das ist unglaublich.

Was ist in Ihrer Familie während der Passion los?
Sehr verrückt: Mein Mann dirigiert, ich singe Alt, meine beiden erwachsenen Töchter singen Sopran, eine assistiert auch noch meinem Mann. Ich freu mich total, mit meinen Töchtern auf der Bühne zu stehen und mit ihnen ein Duett zu singen.

Peter Stückl
* 1942 | Annas und Vater des Spielleiters Christian Stückl
Annas and father of the director Christian Stückl

What is your first memory of the Passion Play?
The frankfurter sausages that my grandpa bought me in the cafeteria of the Passion Play. I can still taste them today. That was back in 1950. Now, this is my tenth Passion Play.

Which parts have you played?
As a child, I was part of the entry into Jerusalem, then I sang bass in the choir. I played Caiaphas, Judas, Nathanael, and now Annas, the priest, for the second time. In 1990, Christian's first year as the play director, he asked me if I wanted to play Judas. My wife said: "He'll do it, Christian. Then he kills himself at 3:30 and can be home for coffee and cake after that."

Didn't you ever want to play Jesus?
No, never. That was the most boring part. In earlier years, Jesus didn't have any lines at all in the afternoon, he was only suffering.

What was the Passion Play like in the 1950s and 1960s?
It was extremely Catholic. My mother was a Protestant, and my father a Catholic. He was supposed to play Jesus in 1960, but our priest said, that it was impossible that a man married to a Protestant woman played Jesus. Back then, Protestants were considered to be just as bad as the refugees, who came to town after the war. To prevent them from being part of the play, a new rule was established specifying that new residents had to live in Oberammergau for 20 years before they were allowed to participate in the Passion Play. That's so ridiculous. Back then, it was quite impossible, however, to criticize the church or the Passion Play.

How do you feel about the Catholic Church?
There are many things about the Catholic church that I have always despised. Still, I have never thought about leaving the church. There are so many good priests, but some are arrogant jerks, too – just like everywhere else. Luckily, nowadays, the Passion Play ist not connected to the Church all that strongly anymore.

How have your feelings towards the Passion Play changed over the years?
Today, I think differently about it. In earlier years, the important thing for me was to get a good part in the play. Today I worry about staying healthy and remembering my text. I will be 80 years old soon, so I am not as naive and carefree about acting as I used to be.

Was ist Ihre erste Erinnerung an die Passion?
Die Wiener Würstel vom Opa, die hat er mir in der Passionskantine spendiert. Die schmeck ich heut noch. Das war 1950. Jetzt spiele ich meine zehnte Passion.

Welche Rollen haben Sie schon gespielt?
Ich war als Kind beim Einzug, habe Bass im Chor gesungen, ich war Kaiphas, Judas, Nathanael, und spiele jetzt zum zweiten Mal den Priester Annas. 1990, da war Christian gerade Spielleiter, fragte er mich, ob ich Judas spielen würde. Meine Frau sagte: „Er macht es, Christian, dann bringt er sich um halb vier um und kann dann zum Nachmittagskaffee wieder zu Hause sein."

Hat Sie der Jesus nie gereizt?
Nein, nie. Das war die langweiligste Sache. Jesus hat früher nachmittags überhaupt nichts mehr gesagt, sondern nur noch gelitten.

Wie war die Passion damals, in den 1950er- und 1960er-Jahren?
Furchtbar katholisch. Meine Mutter war evangelisch, mein Vater katholisch. Er hätte 1960 den Christus spielen sollen, aber der Pfarrer sagte, es sei nicht möglich, dass einer, der mit einer evangelischen Frau verheiratet ist, Jesus spielt. Evangelische fand man damals genauso schlimm wie die Geflüchteten, die nach dem Krieg ins Dorf kamen. Damit die nicht mitmachen, hat man damals eingeführt, dass neue Bewohner erst 20 Jahre in Oberammergau leben müssen, bevor sie spielen dürfen. Das ist doch lächerlich. Kritik an der Kirche und der Passion konnte man damals aber nicht wirklich üben.

Wie stehen Sie zur Kirche?
Vieles an der katholischen Kirche hab ich schon immer furchtbar gefunden. Aber austreten habe ich noch nie im Sinn gehabt, es gibt so gute Pfarrer und eben arrogante Trottel, wie halt überall sonst auch. Die Passionsspiele sind heute zum Glück nicht mehr so mit der Kirche verbandelt wie früher.

Wie hat sich Ihre Haltung zur Passion über die Jahre verändert?
Das Denken darüber ist heute anders. Früher war mir wichtig, dass ich eine tolle Rolle kriege. Heute sorge ich mich: Hoffentlich bleibe ich gesund, hoffentlich kann ich mir den Text merken. Ich werde bald 80, da geht man nicht mehr so unbedarft ans Spiel wie früher.

08/2019

02/2020

04/2022

03/2019

08/2019

02/2020

04/2022

02/2020

04/2022

08/2019

Sophie Schuster, Walter Rutz, Kilian Clauss, Rochus Rückel, David Bender und Abdullah Karaca (im Uhrzeigersinn)

Sophie Schuster, Walter Rutz, Kilian Clauss, Rochus Rückel, David Bender and Abdullah Karaca (clockwise)

116 HAIRY AFFAIRS

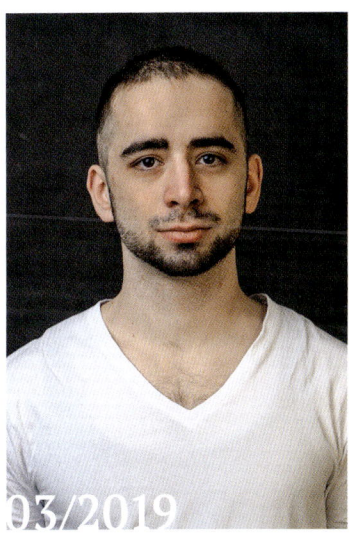 

Haarige Angelegenheit

Was in drei Jahren auf den Köpfen der Spielerinnen und Spieler heranwuchs.

Hairy Affairs

What grew on the heads of the actors and actresses within three years.

Christian Stückl

* 1961 | Spielleiter | *Director*

Anfang April 2022 in Oberammergau. Christian Stückl saß den ganzen Vormittag mit Vertretern der katholischen und evangelischen Kirche zusammen, um über den Eröffnungsgottesdienst zu sprechen, der traditionell vor der Premiere stattfindet. Als er zum Gespräch kommt, seufzt er laut. Mehrmals.

Warum braucht es den Gottesdienst überhaupt noch?
Es gibt viele Menschen, die das Passionsspiel mit der Kirche verbunden sehen, die diesen Gottesdienst brauchen. Ich persönlich bräuchte ihn nicht mehr. Als ich 1990 das erste Mal Spielleiter war, stand das außer Frage. Da gab es sogar zwei Gottesdienste, den zur Gelübde-Erneuerung und den zur Eröffnung. Als ich jung war, hatten wir einen tollen Pfarrer hier. Ich sah mich als Teil der Kirche, die Passionsspiele auch. Dann wurde ich Spielleiter, da kam ein neuer Pfarrer und es wurde schwierig. Ich fing zu streiten an, auch über die Kirche. Also kurz: Als Zwanzigjähriger fühlte ich mich mit der Kirche untrennbar verbunden und als Fünfundzwanzigjähriger war ich mit ihr in ewigem Streit.

Welchen Einfluss hat die katholische Kirche noch? Der sogenannte Patronatsvertrag, den es einst gab, der ist ja abgeschafft.
Das Verrückte ist, diesen Vertrag gab es erst, als ich Spielleiter wurde. Der damalige katholische Pfarrer wollte ein Vertragswerk zu meiner Kontrolle und Mitspracherecht bei der Verteilung der Rollen. Ich sollte unfrei sein. Ein unsäglicher Versuch, einen größeren Einfluss für die Kirche rauszuarbeiten. Der tatsächliche Einfluss war über die Jahrzehnte unterschiedlich, man hat sich aber immer gern vom Bischof den Segen abgeholt. Kardinal Julius Döpfner hat der Passion in den 1970er-Jahren die „Missio Canonica" entzogen, weil sich die Menschen nicht mit dem Antisemitismus im Spiel beschäftigen wollten. Den Missionsauftrag hatte Oberammergau seit den 1930er-Jahren. Weil Hitler die Spiele für „reichswichtig" erklärt hatte, wollte die Kirche da wohl einen spirituellen Gegenpol setzen.

Die katholische Kirche ist nach jüngsten Versäumnissen um die Aufklärung von Missbrauchsfällen in Deutschland an einem Tiefpunkt. Denken Sie über Austritt nach?
Ich bin noch drin, aber warum, weiß ich nicht mehr. Für mich galt immer: So lang ich nicht austrete, also drin bin, darf ich auch kritisieren. Jetzt denke ich, es hat keinen Sinn. Die Kirche wird sich nicht verändern. Es ist aber nicht mal mehr eine Wut in mir da, eher ein Gefühl von Gleichgültigkeit.

Passionsspiele gibt es seit hunderten Jahren. Früher wurden nach dem Spiel oft Pogrome angezettelt. Auch Oberammergau musste, wie Sie sagen, in den 1970er-Jahren sogar von der Kirche gemaßregelt werden, sich dem Antisemitismus zu stellen. Wann haben Sie realisiert, wie viel Antisemitismus im Passionsspiel steckt?
Als ich vielleicht 14 war, lag bei uns zu Hause eine Analyse der Anti-Defamation League und des Jewish Commitee über Antisemitismus in der Passion. Dann sah ich „Holocaust – die Geschichte der Familie Weiß", die Serie hat in den späten 70er-Jahren vielen Menschen die Augen geöffnet und Bilder gezeigt, statt nur diese Riesenzahl von „sechs Millionen" zu nennen. Zur gleichen Zeit habe ich aus dem Schrank Platten mit Klezmermusik rausgezogen und jiddische Lieder auf Partys gesungen, während mein Opa allen Fragen nach Antisemitismus ausgewichen ist. Kurz gesagt: Früh habe ich beides wahrgenommen, Antisemitismus und eine Faszination für das Judentum.

Als Sie Spielleiter wurden, war Ihnen klar, das Thema gehört auf die Agenda?
Ich war 26, ich hatte keine Agenda. Aber in der Beschäftigung mit dem Spiel wurde mir sehr schnell bewusst, wo überall Antisemitismus stecken kann. In den Kostümen etwa. In der Vergangenheit trugen Jesus und seine Apostel öfter Kostüme, die der römischen Ikonografie nahekamen, nicht der jüdischen. Jesus wurde also mit dem „edlen Römer" assoziiert. Wohingegen die Juden eher Kaftan-artige Kostüme trugen.

Der sogenannte „Blutruf", die Stelle aus dem Matthäusevangelium, an der die Juden angeblich die Verantwortung für den Tod Jesus übernehmen, den haben Sie 1990 noch nicht rauslassen dürfen. Ihr damaliger katholischer Aufpasser wollte das so.
Ich habe den Satz den drei ältesten Männern mit Gebiss gegeben, die haben ihn weggenuschelt, sodass ihn kaum einer hörte. Und ich habe das Nuscheln großzügig akzeptiert.

Gibt es die Szene noch, in der das Volk ruft: „Ans Kreuz mit ihm"?
Klar gibt es die, das ist eine der wenigen Möglichkeiten, viele Menschen auf diese Bühne zu bringen. Nur: Der Chor, der für Jesus' Freilassung schreit, wird halt größer. Es gibt nicht das eine Schreien gegen Jesus, sondern eine Vielstimmigkeit.

Early April 2022 in Oberammergau. All morning, Christian Stückl sat and talked to representatives of the Catholic and Protestant church about the opening church service, traditionally held before the premiere. When he enters the room, he sighs loudly. A few times.

Why is the church service still necessary?
There are many people who see a connection between the church and the Passion Play, and they need this service. Me, personally, I wouldn't need it anymore. When I directed the play for the first time, in 1990, there was no question about it. We even had two church services, back then, one for the renewal of the vow and one for the opening. When I was young, we had a great priest here. I saw myself as a part of the church and the Passion Play as well. Then I was elected director and we got a new priest. From then on, it became difficult. I started arguing, also about the church. In a nutshell: when I was 20, I felt inseparably connected to the church, and when I was 25, I was in eternal conflict with it.

What's the influence of the Catholic church today? The so-called patronage agreement has been abolished.
The crazy thing is that this agreement didn't exist before I became director. The new priest back then wanted to have it to control me and have a say in the nomination of the actors. He denied me any freedom. An impossible attempt to increase the influence of the church. Its actual influence varied over the decades, although getting the bishop's blessing was always seen as a nice thing. In the 1970s then, Cardinal Julius Döpfner withdrew the "Missio Canonica" from the Passion Play as people refused to confront the antisemitism in it. Oberammergau had had this mission order since the 1930s. When Hitler declared the Passion Play "important for the Deutsche Reich", the church probably wanted to set a counterpole.

The Catholic church has reached a low point in Germany after its recent failures concerning the clarification of abuse cases. Are you thinking about leaving the church?
I am still a member, but I don't remember why. My rule was: as long as I am a member of the church, I am allowed to criticize it. Now, I think, it's really useless. The church will never change. But by now, I don't feel angry anymore, but rather indifferent.

There have been passion plays for hundreds of years. And there often used to be pogroms afterward. Oberammergau, too, even had to be reproved by the church in the 1970s to face the subject of antisemitism. When did you realize how antisemitic the Passion Play was?
When I was 14, I found an analysis by the Anti-Defamation League and the Jewish Committee of antisemitism in the play lying around at home. Then I watched "Holocaust" – this TV-series was an eye-opener for many people back in the late 1970s; it showed pictures and not only this huge number of "six million". At the same time, I pulled old records of Klezmer music out of the cupboard; and I sang Yiddish songs at parties while my grandfather evaded all questions about antisemitism. So, I felt both very early in my life: antisemitism and a fascination for Judaism.

Did you realize that this subject had to be on your agenda when you were elected director?
I was 26, I didn't have an agenda. But the more I got into the play, the faster I got aware of how much antisemitism can be hidden everywhere. In the costumes, for example. In the past, Jesus and his disciples often wore costumes that were close to the Roman – not the Jewish – iconography. So, Jesus was associated with the "noble Romans." The Jews on the other hand wore rather caftan-like robes.

In 1990, you weren't yet allowed to abolish the so-called "blood curse" from the Gospel of Matthew, where the Jews allegedly take responsibility for the death of Jesus. Your Catholic watchdog wanted it in.
I gave this sentence to the three oldest men on stage, they all had false teeth and mumbled the words so that nobody in the audience really heard them. And I generously accepted that.

Is there still a scene, where the people are shouting: "Crucify him"?
Of course, there is. That's one of the few chances to get many people out on stage. But: the number of people shouting to free Jesus is bigger. There is not this one collective voice shouting against Jesus anymore, but many different voices with different opinions.

Are there other difficult parts, that are not obvious?
In the Gospel of Luke it says, for example: "Woe betide you, you rich." I always understood that as social criticism and thought it was justified. But the line is also

»Die Kirche wird sich nicht verändern.«

»The church will not change.«

Christian Stückl im September 2019 in Caesarea, Israel.

Christian Stückl in September 2019 in Caesarea, Israel.

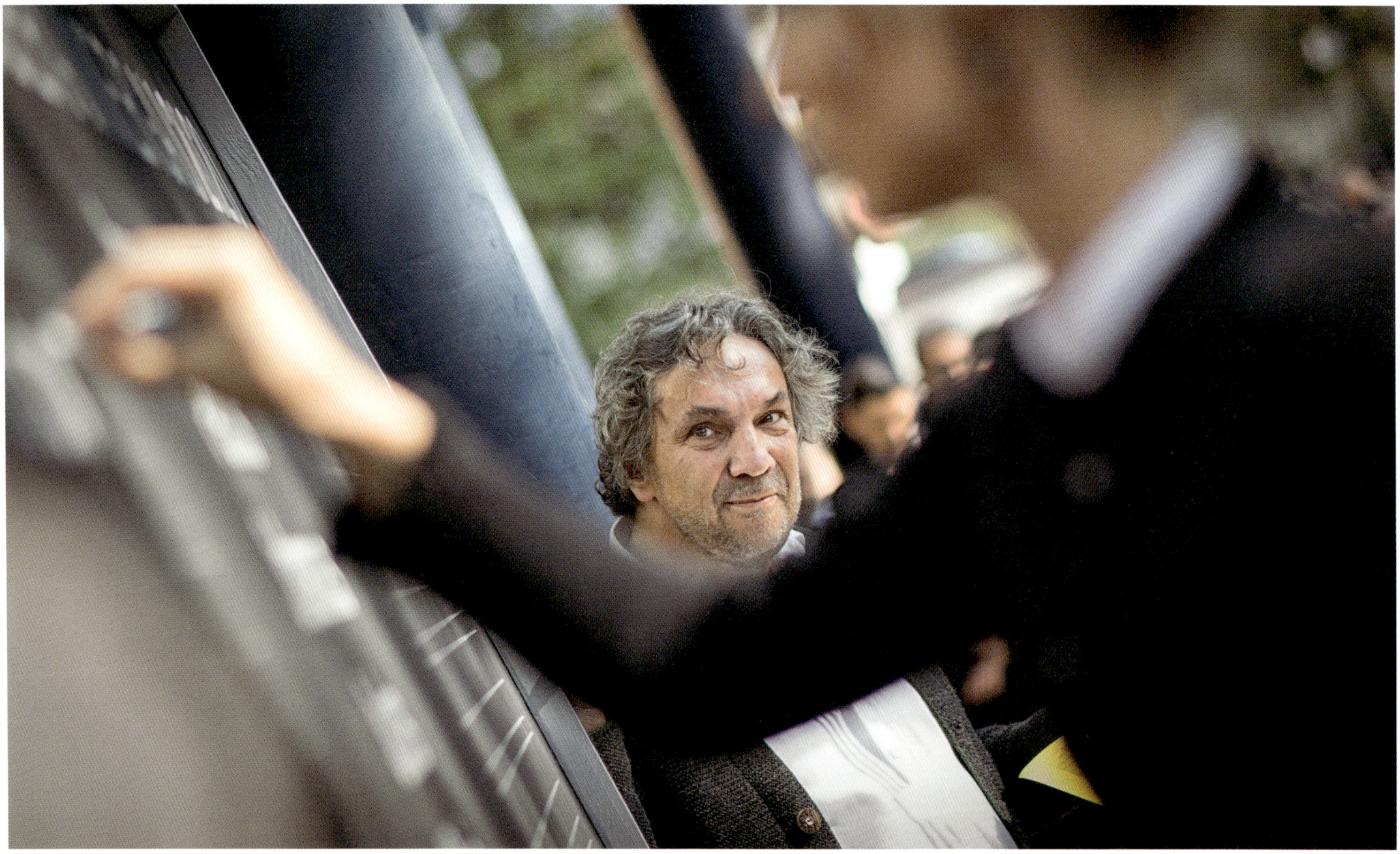

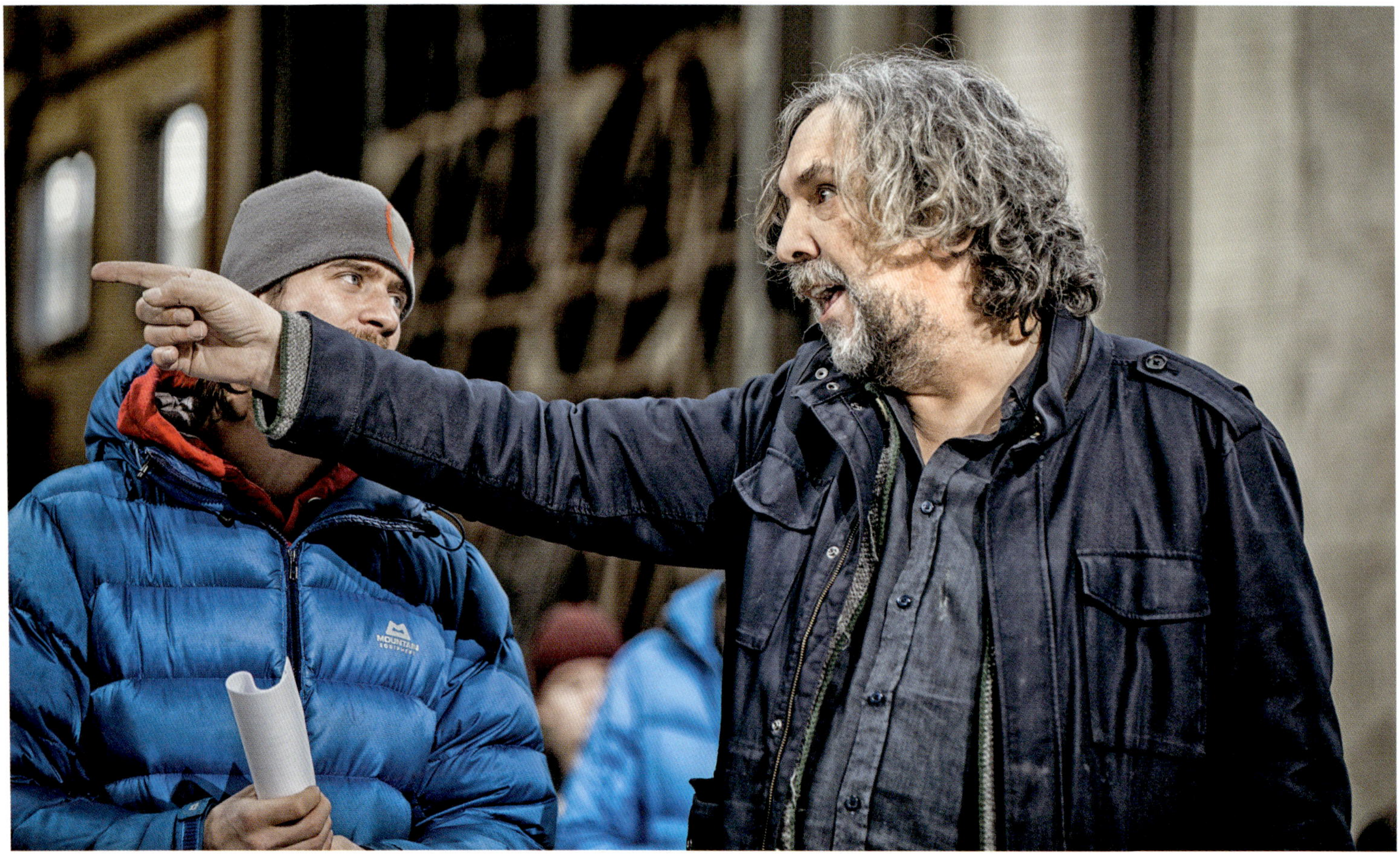

Was ist noch schwierig, vielleicht nicht so offensichtlich?
In der Bibel heißt es, etwa im Lukasevangelium: „Wehe euch, ihr Reichen". Das habe ich immer als Sozialkritik verstanden und fand sie als solche berechtigt. Aber auch der Satz ist problematisch, weil damit Juden als „die Reichen" bezeichnet werden, was wiederum ein antisemitisches Ressentiment ist. Wenn du diese Brille einmal aufsetzt, siehst du hinter jedem Satz potenziellen Antisemitismus, ich bin extrem sensibilisiert. Aber die Geschichte der Verurteilung Jesu ist auch ein innerjüdischer Konflikt und auf der Bühne muss es diesen Konflikt geben. Wenn es keinen Konflikt mehr gibt, dann brauchen wir kein Theater machen.

Wie gehen Sie mit Kaiphas und Pilatus um? Beides mächtige Männer und mutmaßlich an der Verurteilung von Jesus beteiligt, einer Hohepriester und Tempelvorsteher, der andere Statthalter der Römer.
Wenn man die Evangelien anschaut, sieht man sehr gut, was nachträglich konstruiert wurde. Jesus musste sterben, damit sich die Schrift erfüllt. In allen vier Evangelien fragt Pilatus: „Bist du der König der Juden?" Antwort Jesus: „Ja, ich bin es." Auf Jesus' Kreuz stand dann „Iesus Nazarenus Rex Iudaeorum", seine begangene Straftat, sozusagen. Da macht sich einer zum König in einem Land, in dem es keinen König geben darf, weil die Römer darüber herrschen. Die Hinrichtungsart der Kreuzigung ist auch ein Zeichen dafür, dass es die Römer zu verantworten haben. Wenn Jesus vor allem der Gotteslästerung angeklagt gewesen wäre, hätte man ihn wohl eher gesteinigt. So muss man sagen: Er hatte wohl eine Auseinandersetzung mit den Römern, nicht mal unbedingt eine religiöse, sondern eine politische. Historisch gesehen war also Statthalter Pilatus „schuld".

Und Kaiphas?
Jesus zieht in Jerusalem ein, lässt sich mit Palmen bewinken und zettelt auch noch einen, wir würden sagen, Volksaufstand an. Und Kaiphas war von den Römern eingesetzt, als oberster Chef des Tempels für Ruhe zu sorgen. Er sagt im Johannesevangelium: „Ihr bedenkt nicht, dass es besser für euch ist, wenn ein einziger Mensch für das Volk stirbt, als wenn das ganze Volk zugrunde geht." Er will und muss also sein Volk schützen vor dem Aufrührer. Aus Kalkül hat er Jesus also vielleicht sogar ausgeliefert an die Römer. Danach fängt die Schwierigkeit an – wie ging es weiter?

Sie bekommen Preise, auch von jüdischen Organisationen, für Ihr Engagement gegen Antisemitismus und Ihr ernsthaftes Interesse an Austausch. Wie war die Auseinandersetzung mit dem Thema für diese Passion 2022?
Ich inszeniere die Passion jetzt zum vierten Mal und ich höre nie auf, darüber nachzudenken. Aber da gibt es ja wenigstens die Möglichkeit, was voranzubringen, im Gegensatz zur Kirche. Wir waren vor einiger Zeit etwa in New York beim Jewish Committee und bei der Anti-Defamation League, wir haben Vertreter hierher eingeladen, dass sie auf Texte, Kostümentwürfe und Skizzen schauen. Die sagen mir immer: „Christian, ihr werdet nie ein Koscher-Siegel von uns bekommen." Das ist mir klar.

Kann man die Passionsgeschichte überhaupt ohne Antisemitismus erzählen?
Ja, das ist möglich. Trotzdem kann es sein, dass ein Einzelner trotzdem Antisemitismus darin entdeckt.

Was kann dann Ihr Anspruch sein, als Spielleiter?
Mein Anspruch ist klar: Ich will keinen Antisemitismus im Spiel haben. Ob ich das jemals schaffe, weiß ich nicht.

Wenn wir schon beim Interpretieren sind: Es gibt sehr wenige gute Frauenrollen in der Passion. Können Sie sich vorstellen, mal einen Jünger mit einer Frau zu besetzen?
Eigentlich nein. Querbesetzungen am Theater können funktionieren. Wenn in Büchners „Woyzeck" der Arzt eine Frau ist, dann behandle ich das als Regisseur auch so. Wenn beim „Jedermann" der Tod eine Frau ist, ist die Dynamik der Geschichte schon anders: Dann ist neben der Buhlschaft eine weitere Frau da, mit der der Jedermann dann tanzen will, das schafft ganz neue Erzählprobleme. Wäre der Jünger dann ein Mann, den eine Frau spielt? Oder wäre es eine Jüngerin Johanna? Und was hieße das? Ich finde, es braucht eher spannende heutige Stücke mit guten Frauenrollen. Wenn wir einfach alle Männerrollen von Frauen spielen lassen, da kommt doch nichts Gescheites raus.

Gab es nach den zwei Jahren Pause etwas, das Sie neu angeschaut haben und dachten: Himmel, das muss 2022 ganz anders werden!
Das Schlimme ist: fast alles! Zwei Jahre später ist fast alles komisch. Komisch, alles von 2020 wieder aufzugreifen. Ich denke oft, ich müsst noch mal ganz neu anfangen. Was natürlich nicht geht, die gleiche Bühne, die gleiche Besetzung, das fühlt sich teilweise sehr retro an.

problematic because Jews are called "the rich", which again is an antisemitic resentment. Once you take this perspective, you detect potential antisemitism behind every single sentence – I have become very sensitive to that. But the story of Jesus' condemnation is also an inner-Jewish conflict and this conflict must be shown on stage. If there are no conflicts, we don't need to do theatre anymore.

How do you deal with Caiaphas and Pontius Pilate? Both were powerful men and presumably involved in Jesus' condemnation, one of them was a High Priest and temple chief, the other governor of the Romans.
When you investigate the gospels, you see very well, which parts were constructed subsequently. Jesus had to die to fulfill the scriptures. Pontius Pilate asks in all four gospels: "Are you the king of the Jews?" And Jesus answers: "Yes, I am." So, on his cross they put "Iesus Nazarenus Rex Iudaeorum", which was the crime he had committed, so to speak. A man calls himself king of a country that must not have a king because the Romans reign there. The crucifixion as the chosen method of execution also shows that it's the Romans who are responsible for the condemnation. Had Jesus been accused of blasphemy, he probably would have been stoned. So, the thing is: the conflict he had was mostly with the Romans, and it was not necessarily a religious but rather a political one. Historically, Governor Pontius Pilate was to blame for his death.

And Caiaphas?
Jesus enters Jerusalem, lets himself be greeted with palm leaves and even instigates something like a popular upspring. Now, the Romans had made Caiaphas temple chief and he is supposed to make sure everything stays calm. In the gospel of John, he says: "You know nothing at all! You do not realize that it is better for you that one man dies for the people than that the whole nation perishes." He wants to and has to protect his people against the agitator. He might even have surrendered Jesus to the Romans himself driven by calculation. But that's when it gets difficult – what happened next?

You receive many awards, also from Jewish organizations, for your commitment to fight antisemitism and your interest in exchange. How have you confronted this subject for this Passion Play 2022?
This is my fourth time directing the Passion Play, and I will never stop thinking about this. But here, at least I have a chance to change and improve something as opposed to in the church. Some time ago, we visited the Jewish Committee and the Anti-Defamation League in New York; and we also invited representatives here to look over texts, costume and stage designs. They keep telling me: "Christian, you will never get a kosher-seal from us." I am totally aware of that.

Is it possible at all to tell the passion without antisemitism?
Yes, it is. But it can happen, that one individual viewer still detects antisemitism in it.

So, what do you aim for as the director?
That is very clear: I don't want any antisemitism in the Passion Play. But I don't know if I will succeed.

Now, if we are talking interpretation: there are very few good parts for women in the Passion Play. Can you imagine giving the part of a disciple to a woman one day?
Not really. This can work in professional theatre. If in Büchner's play "Woyzeck" the doctor is a woman, I can deal with that as the director. If the part of "death" is a woman in the play "Jedermann", the dynamics of the whole story change. Because we have another female aside from the "Buhlschaft" that Jedermann wants to dance with. And this creates all new problems for telling the story. So, would the disciple be a man played by a woman? Or would it be a female disciple Joan? And what would that mean? In my opinion, we need more modern plays with good parts for women. Giving all male parts to women won't really get us anywhere.

Is there anything that you looked at after the two-year break and said: Oh my, this must be changed completely for 2022!
Almost everything – that's a real problem! Two years later, almost everything sounds and looks funny. And it feels strange to go back to the things as we left them in 2020. I often think I should start over completely. Which is not possible, of course. We have the same stage and the same cast, but sometimes it has a real retro feel to it.

The conditions for the Passion Play aren't any better now than they were in 2020.
Two years ago, maybe the world was still a little better. Now, everything seems so messed up, that I wonder how we can possibly do justice to this world with what we do on stage. Deep inside, I sometimes think: Is this story still relevant today? Very strange.

Dinge abgeben? Nur, wenn's sein muss.
Der Spielleiter bei einer Leseprobe.

*Delegating things? Only if it's absolutely necessary.
The director during a reading rehearsal.*

Why do you go through all of this, then?
Because there are such great moments and such great people here. Because we put something great on stage together. I just got out of the hospital after four days of treatment. There, the doctors told me, how important it is, to take better care of myself and my body. But why? To spend all your time looking inside of yourself and waste away like all the others around you? And to miss what is going on in the world? No, I am still burning, just as I did before. And if that means it's over faster, then that's how it is.

In late February 2022, Christian Stückl suffers a small heart attack and has to be hospitalized. All of Oberammergau is in shock. After four days, he is released. With stents and the firm intention to give up smoking. From 80 cigarettes a day down to zero. Stückl grins, pulls a wooden cigarette out of his breast pocket and sticks it into his mouth: "Got a light?"

Has this incision changed your life?

He holds up the wooden cigarette.

I do understand that I should stop this right now. And I am glad that there are all these surgical solutions – they put in a stent, and everything is back to normal. But I should have gone to rehab. There they help you quit smoking, there is a food plan, you do yoga – total re-education measures. But, I don't want to be re-educated; I feel totally fine. So, I didn't go.

*Do you ever think about letting go of all of this?
It is obviously hard for you to delegate things.*
He turns to his assistant Kilian Clauss: Why don't you ask him, how much work he has to do? I stay out of that completely. Kilian? I do delegate a lot!

Kilian Clauss: Well, it would make a lot of work steps easier, if you didn't have to re-check and sign off on everything …

A short discussion ensues about who is responsible for what and when. No agreement is reached.

Stückl: I do delegate a lot! But I also admit that staging and directing are things that I still prefer doing myself.

And who will be the director of the Passion Play in 2030?
That is a good question.

You, maybe?
I don't worry about that right now. We have seen how fast things can change. You can have a heart attack and that's it then.

Die Bedingungen, unter denen die Passion jetzt stattfindet, die sind jedenfalls nicht besser als 2020.
Vielleicht war die Welt aber in sich noch etwas mehr in Ordnung vor zwei Jahren. Jetzt scheint gerade alles derart durcheinander, dass ich mich frage, wie wir dieser Welt gerecht werden können mit dem, was wir auf dieser Bühne machen. Ganz tief drin kommen mir manchmal die Gedanken: Hat die Geschichte noch Relevanz in unserer Zeit? Eigenartig.

Warum tun Sie sich das alles dann an?
Na, weil es so schöne Momente und so tolle Menschen hier gibt. Weil wir zusammen was auf die Beine stellen. Ich war gerade vier Tage im Krankenhaus. Da haben mir die Ärzte erklärt, wie wichtig es ist, dass ich mehr auf meinen Körper und auf mich achte. Warum? Um dann vor lauter Innenschau so herumzusiechen wie alle anderen? Nur noch auf sich schauen und nicht mehr mitkriegen, was draußen passiert? Nein, ich brenn genauso weiter wie in der Vergangenheit, und wenn es dann schneller rum ist, ist es halt schneller rum.

Ende Februar 2022 erleidet Christian Stückl einen kleinen Herzinfarkt und muss ins Krankenhaus. Ganz Oberammergau erschrickt. Nach vier Tagen darf er wieder raus. Mit Stents und dem festen Vorsatz, nicht mehr zu rauchen. Von 80 Zigaretten täglich auf null. Stückl grinst, greift in seine Brusttasche und holt eine Holzzigarette heraus, steckt sie in den Mund: „Hast du mal Feuer?"

Hat dieser Einschnitt Ihr Denken verändert?

Er wedelt mit der Holzzigarette.

Ich verstehe ja, dass ich das hier momentan lieber bleiben lassen sollte. Und ich bin froh, dass es diese medizinischen Möglichkeiten gibt, da setzen sie dir einen Stent ein und dann geht die Pumpe wieder. Aber ich hätte in die Reha gehen sollen. Da gewöhnen sie dir das Rauchen ab, es gibt einen Essensplan und du machst Yoga, totale Umerziehungsmaßnahme. Ich will aber gar nicht umerzogen werden, ich fühle mich total okay. Also bin ich nicht hin.

Wie denken Sie über Loslassen nach? Sie tun sich offenbar schwer mit Delegieren und Abgeben.
Er wendet sich seinem Assistenten Kilian Clauss zu:
Fragen Sie mal den, wie viel er machen muss, da leg ich absolut die Füße hoch. Kilian? Ich gebe schon viel ab!

Kilian Clauss: Na ja, es würde einige Arbeitsprozesse erleichtern, wenn du nicht überall deinen Haken drunter setzen müsstest …

Es entspinnt sich ein kleines Gespräch, wer wofür wann zuständig ist und wofür nicht. Ausgang unentschieden.

Stückl: Ich gebe viel ab! Aber ich gebe ganz ehrlich zu: Nur das Inszenieren mach ich noch lieber selbst!

Und wer inszeniert die Passion 2030?
Das würde mich wirklich auch interessieren.

Sie vielleicht?
Da mach ich mir keine Gedanken. Sie sehen ja, wie schnell es gehen kann. Da hast du einen Herzinfarkt und schon bist du weg.

Ob er 2030 noch mal ran will?

Will he do it again in 2030?

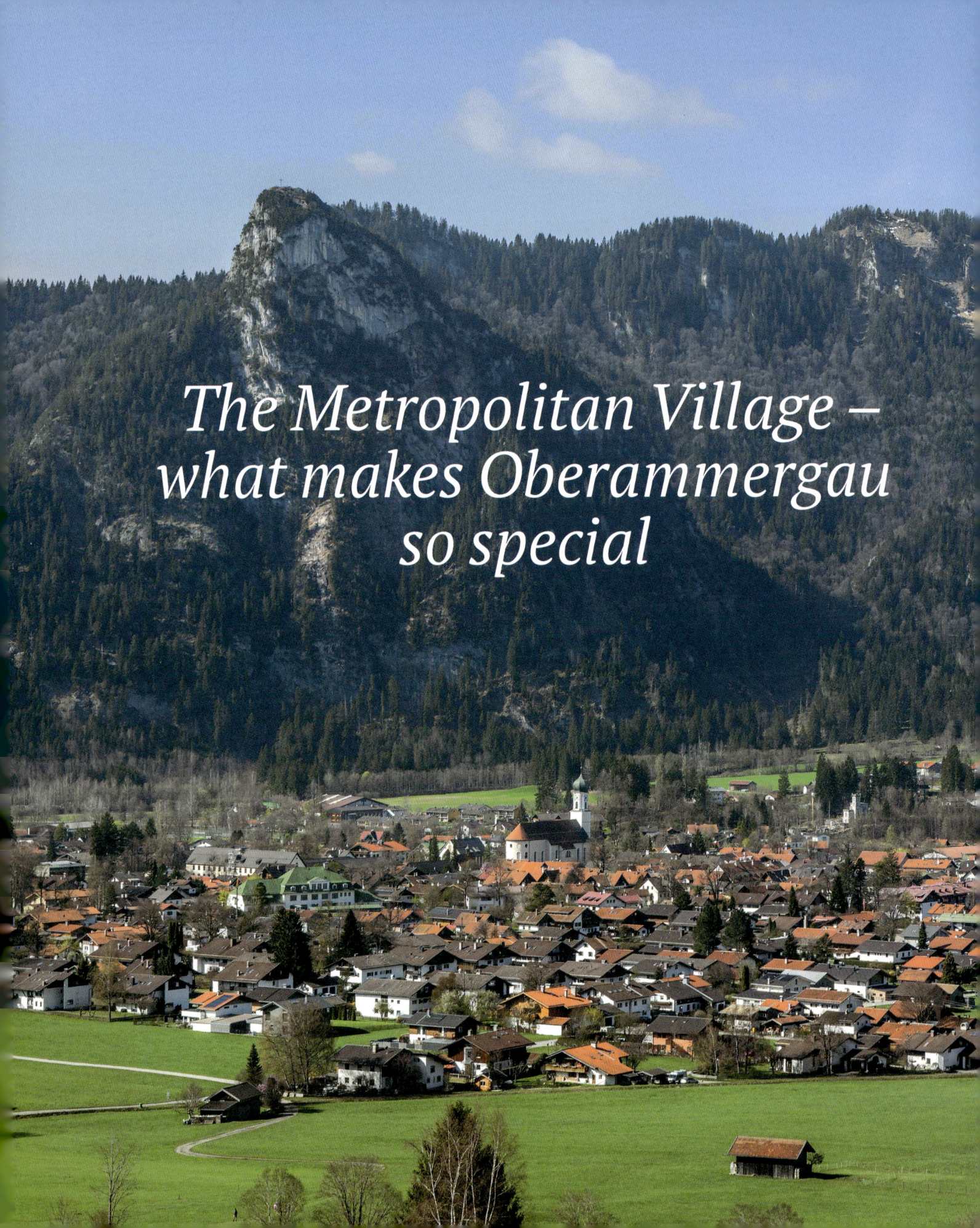

The Metropolitan Village – what makes Oberammergau so special

Ein Dorf von Welt – Was Oberammergau so besonders macht

What is it that makes Oberammergau so different from other villages? The Passion Play, of course. And it also influences local politics as well as the atmosphere in town.

Written by Matthias Köpf

Andrea Hecht war schon als Kind Fan von der Maria, nun spielt sie sie selbst.

Andrea Hecht was a fan of Mary when she was a child; now she plays Mary herself.

Everybody in Oberammergau remembers their first Passion Play, and everybody has his or her own special memories. One of the locals remembers waiting at the train station in 1950 with a handcart to pick up Passion Play guests and their luggage. Another one still sees himself in the arms of his grandfather and looking up at his father who played a Roman captain and waved at him from his horse. One woman remembers "being a great fan of Mary" when she was a little girl.

This woman is called Andrea Hecht, and now she plays Mary herself – for the third time in a row, in fact. Her first main part was Mary Magdalene in 1990, but she started like most of her fellow actors as an extra in the crowd when she was just a little girl. "I will never stand on a stage and talk in front of so many people," she thought back then. But then, when it was time for her, it felt very good and very special, she continues. The Passion Play is "the biggest social event that we have here," says Andrea Hecht standing in her small shop near the Passion Play Theatre. "Everybody must be in to put all this on stage."

Still, the rules have changed a bit over time for Oberammergau and its 5,400 inhabitants. Until Stückl was nominated as director in 1987, only Catholics were allowed to be on stage; women had to be unmarried and younger than 35. Some women went to court, and in February 1990 the Bavarian Administrative Court decided that women could not be denied the right to vote in the Passion Play Committee and the right to play due to their marital status or their age. When Stückl gave the first main part in the play to a protestant in 1990, the Catholic priest collected 1,800 signatures against it. The people from Oberammergau may be much more familiar with the New Testament due to their Passion Play than people elsewhere in Bavaria. But that doesn't make them any more religious. Andrea Hecht, too, sees it that way: "The Passion Play gives the people a lot of opportunity to think about their own faith but also about all the doubts they have about it," she says. And sometimes, it seems as if the good Lord has taken away the plague from the Oberammergau people but has also struck them with the eternal dispute. If something is of such enormous importance for a town and its residents, then there is bound to be a variety of different opinions about it. "Because everyone wants to do the best he or she can", says Andrea Hecht. But sometimes, people don't agree on what is best. So, the residents are used to conflicts and debates. There have been public petitions for and against certain candidates for the job as director, for and

Überall im Ort findet man geschnitzte Figuren, mal mehr, mal weniger hochwertig.

Everywhere in town, one can see carved figures – some more, and some less high-quality.

Was Oberammergau von anderen Orten unterscheidet? Die Passion natürlich. Und die wirkt auch in die Lokalpolitik und die Stimmung des ganzen Dorfes.

Von Matthias Köpf

An ihre erste Passion erinnern sie sich alle in Oberammergau, ein jeder an seine eigene. So weiß der eine noch gut, wie er 1950 mit dem Leiterwagen Passionsgäste samt Gepäck vom Bahnhof abgeholt hat. Ein anderer sieht sich noch selbst als kleinen Jungen auf dem Arm des Großvaters, wie ihm der Vater als römischer Hauptmann hoch vom Pferd herunter zuwinkt. Und eine Dritte erinnert sich, dass sie schon als Kind „ein Fan von der Maria" war.

Diese Dritte heißt Andrea Hecht und spielt die Maria längst selbst, und das schon zum dritten Mal in Folge. Ihre erste Hauptrolle war 1990 die Magdalena, doch angefangen hat Andrea Hecht wie die meisten Mitspieler als Kind und als Statistin im Volk. „Ich geh nicht auf eine Bühne und rede vor den Leuten", dachte sie sich als kleines Mädchen. Aber als es dann so weit war, da sei es eben doch etwas ganz Schönes und Besonderes gewesen. Die Passion ist „der größte soziale Event, den wir haben", sagt Andrea Hecht in ihrem kleinen Laden in der Nähe des Passionstheaters. „Das auf die Bühne zu stellen, das braucht einfach einen jeden."

Wer „ein jeder" ist im 5400-Einwohner-Ort Oberammergau, das hat sich mit der Zeit aber verändert. Bis Christian Stückl 1987 Spielleiter wurde, durften nur Katholiken mitspielen, Frauen nur unverheiratet und jünger als 35. Ein paar Frauen klagten, der Bayerische Verwaltungsgerichtshof entschied im Februar 1990, den Frauen dürfe das Wahlrecht zum Passionsspielkomitee und das Mitwirkungsrecht am Spiel nicht wegen ihres Familienstandes oder ihres Alters verweigert werden. Und als Stückl 1990 die erste Hauptrolle mit einem Protestanten besetzte, sammelte der katholische Pfarrer 1800 Unterschriften dagegen. Die Oberammergauer mögen wegen ihrer Passion mit dem Neuen Testament deutlich vertrauter sein als die Menschen anderswo in Bayern. Doch frömmer sind sie deswegen nicht. Auch Andrea Hecht schätzt die Lage ähnlich ein: Man habe durch die Passion zwar sehr viel Gelegenheit, sich mit seinem Glauben auseinanderzusetzen, aber zugleich auch mit all seinen Zweifeln. Zweifel an der Passion gibt es hingegen weniger. 2022 wirken mehr als ein Drittel der Einwohner in irgendeiner Weise mit. Viele kalkulieren Jahre im Voraus, wie sich das etwa mit einer Ausbildung oder einem Studium vereinbaren lässt. Wer es mit dem Arbeitgeber einrichten kann, nimmt unbezahlten Urlaub, was vor allem für die Hauptrollen auch kaum anders geht. Dafür gibt es ein Honorar von der Gemeinde, das einem Vollzeitjob angemessen ist.

Die große Gemeinsamkeit, welche die Passion im Ort stiftet, ist die eine Seite. Auf der anderen scheint es

Die katholische Sankt Peter und Paul Kirche.

The Catholic church St. Peter and Paul.

against the roofing or reconstruction of the stage, for and against the extension of the play into the evening hours. This last point Stückl fought through for the Passion Play in 2010, because he wanted to make the crucifixion scenes more effectful. More than twelve local referendums have been held since these were introduced in Bavaria in 1995 – more than practically anywhere else in the region and by far the most per capita.

Everyone in Oberammergau wants to have a say, there are referendums all the time

Being on stage and performing in front of more than 4,000 people probably strengthen people's self-confidence in terms of local politics, too. The local council with its 20 members sometimes consisted of up to nine different political groups. Now there are five different parties represented in the council – "only five," says mayor Andreas Rödl from the conservative party. He sounds relieved.

One man who has a say in town and in the local council is Anton Preisinger. He used to be the little boy who watched his father on the horse from the arms of his grandfather. This was back in 1970, and the grandfather was the director at the time after his predecessor had resigned because of a dispute about the correct text version. By now, the little boy has grown up – and has grown a long beard himself several times. In 1990 he played Archelaus, in 2000 he was Judas, and in 2010 he was Caiaphas, one of the largest speaking parts next to Jesus. This year, he didn't have to grow a beard because he plays the traditionally beardless Roman Pontius Pilate. "An advantage," he says. The disadvantage: His guests probably won't approach him quite as often to ask about his role in the play.

Anton Preisinger betreibt das Hotel "Alte Post" (rechts). Andreas Rödl wurde kurz vor der Absage 2020 zum neuen Bürgermeister gewählt (rechts unten).

Anton Preisinger runs the hotel „Alte Post" (right). Andreas Rödl was elected as the new mayor shortly before the Passion Play was canceled in 2020 (bottom right).

manchmal fast so, als ob ihr Herrgott den Oberammergauern damals zwar die Pest vom Hals gehalten, sie dafür aber auch mit ewigem Streit geschlagen hätte. Denn wenn etwas so wichtig wird für ein Dorf und seine Menschen, dann gehen die Ansichten darüber auch schnell auseinander. „Weil es jeder so gut machen will, wie er kann", sagt Andrea Hecht. Aber jeder kann und will es eben manchmal anders als die anderen, weshalb die Oberammergauer mindestens das Debattieren gewohnt sind. So gab es schon Bürgerbegehren für diesen und gegen jenen Kandidaten für das Spielleiter-Amt, für und gegen eine Überdachung oder einen Umbau der Bühne, für und gegen die Ausdehnung des Spiels in den Abend hinein. Das setzte Stückl für die Passion 2010 durch, wohl auch, um die Wirkung der Kreuzigungsszene zu verstärken. Ein gutes Dutzend Bürgerentscheide wurden schon abgehalten, seit sie 1995 bayernweit eingeführt wurden – mehr als praktisch überall sonst und auf jeden Fall mit Abstand die meisten pro Kopf.

In Oberammergau wollen die Leute mitreden, ständig gibt es Bürgerentscheide

Vor mehr als 4000 Menschen auf einer Bühne aufzutreten, stärkt womöglich auch das lokalpolitische Selbstbewusstsein. Im 20 Mitglieder starken Gemeinderat gab es zeitweise neun verschiedene politische Gruppen. Derzeit sind es fünf – „nur", sagt Bürgermeister Andreas Rödl von der CSU mit einer gewissen Erleichterung.

Einer, der mitredet im Ort und im Gemeinderat, ist Anton Preisinger. Er war einst jener kleine Bub, der vom Arm des Großvaters aus den Vater auf dem Pferd beobachtet hat. Die Szene spielte 1970, und der Großvater war damals Spielleiter, nachdem der Vorgänger im Streit über die richtige Textfassung zurückgetreten war. Dem kleinen Buben von damals ist längst schon mehrere Male ein langer Bart gewachsen, 1990 für die Rolle des Archelaus, 2000 als Judas oder 2010 als Kaiphas, eine der größten Sprechrollen neben der des Jesus. Diesmal musste er sich überhaupt keinen Bart wachsen lassen,

EIN DORF VON WELT

Das Oberammergau Museum (rechts) ist für eine Kunstausstellung passend mit alten Passionsgewändern eingekleidet. Es liegt zentral an der Dorfstraße (unten).

To suit the occasion, the Oberammergau Museum (right) has been decorated with old Passion Play robes. It is located in the Dorfstraße (below) in the center of town.

Without its good marketing the Passion Play would not be quite so famous

Anton Preisinger owns a hotel; his family operates the "Alte Post" in the fifth generation. During the years of the Passion Play, all 38 rooms are booked out, of course. And the tables in the restaurant, too, will be occupied up to the last seat every single night of the 110 performance days. But the "Alte Post" and also all the other hotels and restaurants – which are quite a few for a town as small as Oberammergau – are quite well occupied all year round and every year, Passion Play or not. And this is mainly due to the fact that the town is so well known all over the whole world for its Passion Play. Every ten years, however, demand is especially high, and the rooms and holiday flats go for extra high prices. Anton Preisinger likes the special "arrangements": travel packages consisting of an overnight stay in a hotel, a theatre ticket, and dinner. These are marketed by a municipal organization. Such an arrangement can cost several hundred Euros – depending on the hotel and ticket categories.

The numerous guests from the US and Great Britain especially prefer booking such arrangements, often as one component of a longer trip through Europe. To keep it that way, delegations from Oberammergau regularly travel to the US to promote the most famous "product" of the town. Domestically, too, the marketing machine runs at full speed two years before the premiere at the latest. The town owes it mainly to a Baptist priest and tourism pioneer from England that its Passion Play has developed into an international mass tourism event: In 1880, Thomas Cook visited the Passion Play himself, as one of 100,000 viewers even back then. And he immediately recognized its international marketing potential. 25 years later, the railway from Murnau up to the remote Ammertal valley was the first to be electrified in all of Germany.

So, maybe it's not only the famous vow made in 1633, but just this mass tourism marketing that causes the people of Oberammergau to stage their Passion Play again and again up to today. After all, back in the Baroque era countless promises were made to the dear Lord by people and villages all over the country. There were hundreds of passion plays in the German Alpine region. But it was just this one passion play in Oberammergau that has developed into an event, a brand name known all over the world.

denn er spielt den traditionell bartlosen Römer Pontius Pilatus. „Ein Vorteil", wie er sagt. Nachteil: Seine Gäste werden ihn dieses Mal vielleicht nicht ganz so oft auf seine Rolle ansprechen.

Ohne das gute Marketing wäre die Passion wohl nur halb so berühmt

Denn Anton Preisinger ist Hotelier, die Familie betreibt die Alte Post in fünfter Generation. Natürlich sind alle 38 Zimmer in Passionsjahren ausgebucht, und auch die Tische im Restaurant werden sich an jedem der 110 Spieltage füllen bis auf den letzten Platz. Die Alte Post und auch die anderen, für ein Dorf dieser Größe recht zahl- und bettenreichen, Hotels füllen sich dank der Bekanntheit des Ortes auch ohne Passion ganz gut. Aber alle zehn Jahre ist die Nachfrage eben besonders hoch und die Zimmer und Ferienwohnungen lassen sich für ganz andere Preise vermieten. Anton Preisinger setzt auf die „Arrangements" – feste Pakete aus Übernachtung, Eintritt und Essen, die über eine gemeindeeigene Gesellschaft vermarktet werden. Etliche hundert Euro kann so ein Arrangement schon kosten – ganz nach gewählter Hotel- und Platzkategorie.

Die zahlreichen Gäste aus den USA und Großbritannien buchen mit Vorliebe solche Arrangements, oft als Baustein einer größeren Europareise. Damit das so bleibt, reisen wiederum regelmäßig Oberammergauer Delegationen in die USA, um für das berühmteste Produkt der Gemeinde zu werben. Auch im Inland läuft die Marketing-Maschinerie spätestens zwei Jahre vor der Premiere auf hohen Touren. Die Passion als internationales massentouristisches Ereignis haben die Oberammergauer einem baptistischen Geistlichen und Tourismuspionier aus England zu verdanken: Thomas Cook hatte die Passion 1880 als einer von damals schon 100 000 Zuschauern selbst besucht und schnell ihr internationales Vermarktungspotenzial erkannt. 25 Jahre später war ausgerechnet die Bahnlinie von Murnau bis hinauf ins abgelegene Ammertal elektrifiziert, als allererste in ganz Deutschland mit der bis heute gebräuchlichen Stromtechnik.

Und vielleicht ist ja doch nicht das stets wiederholte Gelübde von 1633, sondern genau diese massentaugliche Vermarktung der wahre Grund dafür, dass es die Ober-

Alles überstrahlend: das Passionstheater.

The Passion Play Theatre dominates the view of the town.

When the Passion Play was canceled, the town was hit in two ways: no play and no guests

The town benefits enormously from the 500,000 paying guests that come there during the Passion Play years. The theatre has 4,400 seats and the profit zone starts at an occupancy rate of two-thirds. Up until now, most performances have been sold out over the years, and so the town has been able to treat itself to things that it could otherwise hardly afford in the long run. The large public pool, for example, a huge health and rehab center, newly renovated museums, and the stage roof as it can get quite cold in winter in the theatre – all this sums up to a considerable infrastructure for such a small town. Mayor Andreas Rödl knows that. After the last Passion Play year, 25 million Euros went straight into the municipal coffers.

So, the cancellation of the Passion Play in 2020 hit the town really hard. And hotel owner Anton Preisinger is not so sure anymore, if the next play in 2022 will fix everything. Andrea Hecht, too, expands the product range in her small shop with the usual merchandising products again: Passion Play T-shirts, key rings, blankets, rain coats and badges. But for safety reasons, viewers are not allowed anymore to bring large bags into the theatre.

Who knows, maybe this will keep them from buying souvenirs. These aren't as sought after anymore, anyway. These days, a quick post on Instagram is the best proof of a visit to Oberammergau. People like Andrea Hecht and Anton Preisinger show, how closely life in Oberammergau can be intertwined with the Passion Play. They both play important roles on stage, and they both need the visitors for their businesses. When the Passion Play was canceled in 2020, they were both hit in two ways: They couldn't play and there were no guests, who wanted to spend the night in the hotel "Alte Post" or buy souvenirs in Andrea Hecht's shop. A successful Passion Play season is the key to a lot of things in Oberammergau.

The town is also famous for its numerous woodcarvers. And they, too, can feel that business has gotten tougher. Their shops in town are still countless and can be found at every corner, but still many of them had to close. Even close to the Passion Play Theatre another woodcarver had to give up his shop recently. Andrea Hecht, too, has learned this trade once, just like her siblings, her daughter, and many other relatives. But none of them works as a woodcarver today, she says. Many carvers have changed jobs and work in stage and prop construction now – for the Passion Play.

ammergauer Passion im Jahr 2022 immer noch gibt. Denn damals in der Barockzeit haben die Menschen ihrem Herrgott allerorten viel versprochen, Passionsspiele gab es Hunderte im deutschsprachigen Alpenraum. Doch nur diese eine Passion in Oberammergau ist zur Weltmarke geworden – und wenn die Oberammergauer unter sich sind, dann heißt sie hier immer noch „der Passion" wie einst im Barock.

Als die Passion ausfiel, war das Dorf doppelt getroffen: keine Spiele und keine Übernachtungsgäste

Die Gemeinde profitiert sehr von einer halben Million zahlender Gäste in den Passionsjahren. Mit 4400 Gästen ist das Theater voll, die Gewinnzone beginnt bei einer Auslastung von zwei Dritteln. Aber eigentlich war es ja bisher immer voll, und die Gemeinde hat sich danach dann gerne etwas gegönnt, das sie sich auf Dauer kaum leisten kann. Das große Hallen- und Freibad zum Beispiel, das riesige Kurgästehaus, Museumssanierungen, das Bühnendach, weil es doch recht kalt werden kann im Theater – eine stolze Infrastruktur für ein kleines Dorf, wie auch Bürgermeister Andreas Rödl sagt. 25 Millionen Euro waren zuletzt in so einem Passionsjahr in der Gemeindekasse hängen geblieben – und doch musste schon mehrmals der Staat mit Bürgschaften einspringen, damit die Oberammergauer überhaupt die Vorbereitungen für die nächste Passion bezahlen konnten.

Umso härter hat die pandemiebedingte Verschiebung der Passion den Ort 2020 getroffen. Dass die nächste Passion sowieso alles wieder richten wird, sei aber schon längst nicht mehr gewiss, sagt der Hotelier Anton Preisinger. Auch Andrea Hecht nimmt in ihrem Laden beim Passionstheater wieder die üblichen Merchandising-Artikel ins Sortiment, Passions-T-Shirts zum Beispiel, Schlüsselanhänger, Decken, Regenjacken und Anstecknadeln. Den ganzen Laden dafür freizuräumen, wäre vielleicht einträglicher, sagt sie. Aber nur darauf will sie sich nicht gern verlassen. Aus Sicherheitsgründen dürfen die Besucher inzwischen keine größeren Taschen mehr ins Theater mitnehmen. Wer weiß, ob das nicht die Kauffreude dämpft. Souvenirs sind auch in Oberammergau nicht mehr so gefragt wie früher, als Besuchsnachweis reicht ja auch ein schneller Post auf Instagram.

An Menschen wie Andrea Hecht und Anton Preisinger lässt sich ablesen, wie eng ein Oberammergauer Leben mit der Passion verwoben sein kann. Beide spielen mit, beide brauchen die Passionszuschauer für ihre Geschäfte. Als die Passion 2020 ausfiel, war es für beide doppelt schmerzhaft. Nicht nur spielten sie nicht, es kamen auch keine auswärtigen Gäste, die in der Alten Post übernachten oder in Andrea Hechts Geschäft einkaufen wollten. Vieles steht und fällt in Oberammergau mit einer erfolgreichen Passion.

Auch die zahllosen Holzschnitzer, für die das Dorf ebenfalls berühmt ist, spüren, dass das Geschäft härter geworden ist. Ihre Läden sind zwar immer noch unübersehbar an jeder zweiten Ecke zu finden, aber sie werden weniger. Selbst in nächster Nähe des Passionstheaters hat gerade wieder einer dichtgemacht. Auch Andrea Hecht hat dieses Handwerk einmal gelernt, genau wie ihre Geschwister, ihre Tochter und viele andere Verwandte. Eine Schnitzerei habe von ihnen keiner mehr, erzählt sie. Viele Holzschnitzer führen ihre Kunst inzwischen lieber im Bühnen- oder Requisitenbau weiter – bei den Passionsspielen.

Eine Schülerin der Schnitzschule kopiert eine Büste von Bildhauer Tilman Riemenschneider.

An apprentice in the woodcarving school is copying a bust by the sculptor Tilman Riemenschneider.

Christian Bierling
* 1965 | Josef von Arimathäa | *Joseph of Arimathea*

What do you do when there is no Passion Play?
I do special effects for television and film. A lot of pyrotechnics, rain, wind, snow, shell bursts, body hits – wherever there is blood or explosions.

What do you remember about earlier Passion Plays?
This is my seventh Passion Play. During the 1980s the Passion Play didn't interest me at all. I only took part because I got some money to buy a stereo. The town was divided back then, there were two groups – those who just wanted to copy the same conservative play every ten years and reproduce old photos and postcards. And the others around the director Hans Schwaighofer, who wanted to renew the Passion Play. He didn't win. Oberammergau was artistically irrelevant in 1980. No world press. The audience consisted mainly of hypocritical worshippers and religious eccentrics. The actors had the same attitude, and so the Jesus actors seemed like they had come from another galaxy. From all these disputes then emerged the young generation – and Christian Stückl.

What's the best side effect of the Passion Play?
It merges all generations. The old conservative woodcarver and the 15-year-old youngster are sitting side by side in the canteen drinking coffee and talking about their problems. That's how life should be, isn't it?

Who is Joseph of Arimathea?
Joseph of Arimathea is a well-respected member of Jerusalem's society, and he sympathizes with Jesus. He defends him and reminds people that Jesus never breaks Jewish law. He urges the High Council to act calmly and wisely: "Don't allow yourself to get carried away and act wrongfully!" I think he wants to be a mediator, the fatherly type.

Should the actors take a clear position towards the Catholic church and its failures?
Not at all. I have left the church a long time ago. Our story happens long before the Catholic church existed, Jesus was a Jew. Still, the High Priests and their striving for power do remind me of some Catholic dignitaries.

Was machen Sie, wenn keine Passion ist?
Ich mache Spezialeffekte beim Film. Viel Pyrotechnik, Regen, Wind, Schnee, Granateneinschläge, Körpereinschüsse, überall, wo Blut spritzt oder was explodiert.

Wie sind Ihre Erinnerungen an die Passionen?
Dies ist schon meine siebte Passion. In den 80er-Jahren war die Passion für mich völlig uninteressant. Da war ich nur dabei, weil ich bisschen Geld für eine Stereoanlage bekommen habe. Das Dorf war damals zerstritten. Es gab zwei Lager – die, die einfach dasselbe konservative Spiel alle zehn Jahre kopieren und alte Postkartenbilder nachinszenieren wollten. Und die um den Spielleiter Hans Schwaighofer, die eine Erneuerung der Spiele wollten. Er setzte sich nicht durch. Oberammergau war 1980 künstlerisch bedeutungslos. Nichts mit Weltpresse. Im Publikum waren vor allem bigotte Kirchgänger und religiös Verstiegene. Die Darsteller waren genauso drauf und die Jesusse kamen daher wie vom anderen Stern. Aus diesen Streitereien kam dann die junge Generation hervor – und Christian Stückl.

Was ist der beste Passions-Nebeneffekt?
Die Passionszeit ist eine absolute Verschmelzung aller Generationen. Da sitzen der uralte konservative Schnitzer und die 15-Jährige in der Kantine, trinken Kaffee und tauschen sich über Probleme aus. So wünscht man sich doch das ganze Leben.

Wer ist Josef von Arimathäa?
Josef von Arimathäa ist eine angesehene Person in der Gesellschaft Jerusalems, einer, der mit Jesus sympathisiert. Er verteidigt ihn und erinnert daran, dass Jesus nie das jüdische Gesetz bricht. Er mahnt den Hohen Rat zur Ruhe: „Lasst euch nicht zur Ungerechtigkeit hinreißen!" Ich glaube, er ist einer, der vermitteln will, ein väterlicher Typ.

Sollte man sich als Spieler zur katholischen Kirche und deren Versäumnissen positionieren?
Überhaupt nicht. Ich bin lang ausgetreten. Unsere Geschichte ist ja eine vorkirchliche, Jesus war Jude. Auch wenn mich die Hohen Priester von damals in ihren Machtbestrebungen schon an manche katholischen Würdenträger erinnern.

Acknowledgements

A great thank you goes to Frederik Mayet and Franziska Seher for organizing all visits and interviews, to Christian Stückl and above all to the people of Oberammergau, who let us watch and accompany them. Without their openness, this book would not have been possible.

Christiane Lutz:
My personal thanks go to Johannes Hauner, Florian Zinnecker and Laura Warmbrunn, my sisters and my parents who listened to countless anecdotes and supported the project in their own special way.

Danksagung

Ein großer Dank geht an Frederik Mayet und Franziska Seher fürs Organisieren aller Termine, an Christian Stückl und vor allem an die Menschen von Oberammergau, die uns zuschauen und mitreisen ließen und ohne deren Offenheit dieses Buch nicht möglich gewesen wäre.

Christiane Lutz:
Mein persönlicher Dank gilt Johannes Hauner, Florian Zinnecker und Laura Warmbrunn, meinen Schwestern und meinen Eltern, die zahllose Anekdoten erduldet und das Projekt alle auf ihre Weise unterstützt haben.

Impressum
Imprint

Verantwortlich: Sabine Klingan
Lektorat und Redaktion: Christian Schneider
Übersetzung: Anke Harrer
Layout: Nina Andritzky
Repro: LUDWIG:media
Herstellung: Bettina Schippel
Printed in Slovenia by Couleurs Print & More GmbH

> Sind Sie mit diesem Titel zufrieden? Dann würden wir uns über ihre Weiterempfehlung freuen. Erzählen Sie es im Freundeskreis, berichten Sie Ihrem Buchhändler, oder bewerten Sie bei Onlinekauf. Und wenn Sie Kritik, Korrekturen, Aktualisierungen haben, freuen wir uns über Ihre Nachricht an die Süddeutsche Zeitung Edition c/o Bruckmann Verlag GmbH, Postfach 40 02 09, D-80702 München oder per E-Mail an lektorat@verlagshaus.de

Unser komplettes Programm finden Sie unter verlagshaus24.de/sz-edition

Alle Angaben dieses Werkes wurden von den Autoren sorgfältig recherchiert und auf den neuesten Stand gebracht sowie vom Verlag geprüft. Für die Richtigkeit der Angaben kann jedoch keine Haftung übernommen werden, weshalb die Nutzung auf eigene Gefahr erfolgt. Sollte dieses Werk Links auf Webseiten Dritter enthalten, so machen wir uns die Inhalte nicht zu eigen und übernehmen für die Inhalte keine Haftung.

In diesem Buch wird aus Gründen der besseren Lesbarkeit das generische Maskulinum verwendet. Weibliche und anderweitige Geschlechteridentitäten werden dabei ausdrücklich mitgemeint, soweit es für die Aussage erforderlich ist.

Bildnachweis: Alle Bilder im Innenteil und auf dem Umschlag stammen von Sebastian Beck mit folgenden Ausnahmen: S. 100/101, 104, 105 o. und u., 106 o. und Mi., 108, 109, 110: Scherl/Süddeutsche Zeitung Photo; S. 102, 107, 111: SZ Photo/Süddeutsche Zeitung Photo; S. 103: IMAGNO/Photoinstitut Bonartes/Süddeutsche Zeitung Photo; S. 106 u.: Glasshouse Images/Alamy Stock Foto;

Umschlagvorderseite: Die Kreuzigungsszene, Spielleiter C. Stückl (u.)

Umschlagrückseite: Oberammergau, F. Mayet als Jesus in der Maske, In der „Flügelei", B. Schuster als Maria Magdalena, Unterwegs in Israel (v. li. o. n. re. u.)

Die Deutsche Nationalbibliothek verzeichnet diese Publikation in der Deutschen Nationalbibliografie; detaillierte bibliografische Daten sind im Internet über http://dnb.de abrufbar.

© Genehmigte Sonderausgabe für die
SZ Edition in der Süddeutsche Zeitung GmbH

© 2022 SZ Edition in der
Bruckmann Verlag GmbH
Infanteriestraße 11a
80797 München

ISBN 978-3-7343-2650-9

Fotostrecke: Die Vorbereitungen (S. 8-25)
Photo series: The Preparations (p. 8-25)

Herbst 2018: Vor dem Passionstheater findet die Spielerverkündung statt.
Fall 2018: The announcemet of the parts in front of the Passion Play Theatre.

Erschöpfte Pilger am See Genezareth, September 2019.
Exhausted pilgrims at the Sea of Galilee, September 2019.

Hängt da ein Jesus oder kann das weg? Erste Hängeprobe von Frederik Mayet, Februar 2020.
Is this Jesus on the cross or can we put it away? First hanging rehearsal for Frederik Mayet, February 2020.

Das Lebende Bild „Erniedrigung der Israeliten".
The living picture "Degradation of the Israelites".

Frederik Mayet bei der Probe der sogenannten „Geißelung" von Jesus.
Frederik Mayet rehearsing the so-called "flagellation" of Jesus.

Making of Jesus: Frederik Mayet in der Maske.
Making of Jesus: Frederik Mayet getting make-up.

Wie immer? Fast. Erste Proben in Pandemiezeiten.
As usual? Not quite. First rehearsals in times of the pandemic.

Gut ausgeleuchtet: Für Aufnahmen zu einem Fotoband wird die Kreuzigungsszene eingerichtet.
Well illuminated: the crucifixion scene is prepared for pictures for the photo book.

Oberammergauer Pietà: Maria (Andrea Hecht), Jesus (Rochus Rückel), Johannes (Christoph Stöger) und der Heizlüfter.
Pietà Oberammergau-style: Mary (Andrea Hecht), Jesus (Rochus Rückel), John (Christoph Stöger) and the fan heater.

Fotostrecke: Endlich auf der Bühne (S. 140-159)
Photo series: Finally on Stage (p. 140-159)

Das Lebende Bild „Moses und der brennende Dornbusch".
The living picture "Moses and the burning bush".

Einzug nach Jerusalem: Jesus (Frederik Mayet) auf dem Passions-Esel Aramis.
Entry into Jerusalem: Frederik Mayet on the Passion Play donkey Aramis.

Jesus (Rochus Rückel) vertreibt die Händler aus dem Tempel.
Jesus (Rochus Rückel) expels the merchants from the temple.

Das letzte Abendmahl.
The Last Supper.

Was ist von diesem Jesus zu halten? Kritische Blicke des Hohen Rates. In der Mitte: Peter Stückl, Vater des Spielleiters, als Annas.
What shall we make of this Jesus? Critical glances from the members of the High Council. In the center: Peter Stückl, father of the director, as Annas.

Jesus (Rochus Rückel) trägt das Kreuz.
Jesus (Rochus Rückel) is carrying the cross.

Maria (Andrea Hecht) trauert um ihren Sohn. Johannes (Anton Preisinger) gibt Trost.
Mary (Andrea Hecht) is greaving her son. John (Anton Preisinger) offers comfort.

Es ist vollbracht. Kreuzigungsszene vor Oberammergauer Nachthimmel.
All is done. Crucifixion scene against the Oberammergau night sky.

Jesus (Rochus Rückel), mit Maria (Eva Reiser) und Johannes (Anton Preisinger).
Jesus (Rochus Rückel), with Mary (Eva Reiser) and John (Anton Preisinger).

Sophie Schuster als Maria Magdalena.
Sophie Schuster as Mary Magdalene.

Endlich: Die Premiere am 14. Mai 2022 – vor vollbesetztem Haus.
Finally: The premiere on May 14th, 2022 – to a full house.